'A fantastic read, full of humo... ...
bloke from Barnsley who wanted to become a footballer
without the diet sheet. Couldn't put this down,
and had me laughing out loud.'

'Up front, honest and an enjoyable alternative to the Messis
and Ronaldos of this world. I thoroughly enjoyed it.'

'This is a no-holds-barred book with a very gritty level to it.
If he looked after himself better nutrition-wise his life would
have been very boring. Good player – better eater
and drinker though!'

'Sometimes books like this from the lesser known players
(sorry Jon) are way more honest and ultimately more
enjoyable than the ex-Premier League megastars. This was a
quick and fun read with a few laugh-out-loud moments too.'

'Great insight into the game outside the pampered
Premier League for a professional footballer. A character that
every grass roots fan and player can relate to.
Plus, it is very honest and funny.'

'Great read, so honest to hear what really goes on in a
player's life. Once I started, I couldn't put it down.'

'This is such a funny read from a true grassroots footballer.
Plenty of laughs along the way and also real honesty at the
health issues, loneliness and unhappiness football can bring.'

With more than 200 goals in a career spanning around 20 years, Jon Parkin is one of the biggest characters in English football.

His story is one of a natural goalscorer whose talent is always in demand. His unconventional frame and liking for a lager or ten meant pre-season was always a struggle. His straight-talking style and knack of finding himself in trouble resulted in countless bust-ups with managers. But when patience, cash or contracts ran out, there was always another club ready to take a chance on him.

Along the way there have been battles with booze, betting and depression, plus marital breakdown.

There's also been plenty of mischief. One holidaymaker in Magaluf won't easily forget what she found in Parkin's bath.

The Barnsley lad had made his league debut for his hometown club before going on to play for Hartlepool United, York City, Macclesfield Town, Hull City, Stoke City, Preston North End, Cardiff City, Doncaster Rovers, Huddersfield Town, Scunthorpe United, Fleetwood Town, Forest Green Rovers and Newport County.

Success along the way has included promotion with Stoke and Fleetwood, plus an FA Trophy victory with York.

Parkin has collaborated on this book with author David Clayton.

Reach Sport

FEED THE BEAST

JON PARKIN

With DAVID CLAYTON

Forewords by Jilly Cooper and Tony Pulis

For Mum, Dad, brother James and my son Oliver (who won't be reading this until he's 18) for all the support and love shown throughout my journey so far... and for Lucy for all the sacrifices she's made for us to be together x

Reach **Sport**

w w w . r e a c h s p o r t . c o m

Written with David Clayton.

Paperback edition first published in Great Britain and Ireland in 2019 by Reach Sport, 5 St Paul's Square, Liverpool, L3 9SJ. Hardback edition first published 2018.

www.reachsport.com
@reach_sport

Reach Sport is a part of Reach plc.
One Canada Square, Canary Wharf, London, E15 5AP.

1

Paperback ISBN: 978-1-911613-30-5.
Hardback ISBN: 978-1-910335-99-4.
eBook ISBN: 978-1-911613-23-7.

Photographic acknowledgements:
Jon Parkin personal collection, PA Images.

Design and typesetting by Reach Sport.
Editing and production: Simon Monk & Roy Gilfoyle.
Cover design: Calum Cooke.

Printed and bound by CPI Group (UK) Ltd,
Croydon, CR0 4YY.

Contents

ACKNOWLEDGEMENTS

By Jon Parkin, July 2018

There's a few, so here goes. Thanks to the following…

Mum, Dad and James for their constant support. I wouldn't have been able to do it without them and as you will read, they have had to put up with a lot of shit over the years!

For my son, Oliver, who, as the dedication says, won't be reading this any time soon!

For Lucy, my girlfriend, rock and soulmate – for putting up with me and leaving her job and home to live with me in the tropical paradise that is Barnsley.

I also need to thank one of the most important people in my career – my agent Tim Webb. I met Tim with my dad when I was 17 and he told me that he would do everything he could to look after me. Of course, all agents tell you this but in Tim's case it was very true. I've probably bought him that villa in Portugal, but he deserves it. We've had some rough times along the way but he has always been at the end of the phone giving me advice and guiding me as to what is best to do and for that I will be forever grateful. Cheers Tim.

To my best mate Jamie. What can I say? We've had some adventures over the years and I was honoured to be asked to be your best man. For looking out for me on nights out when things could have turned sour (through no fault of my own), for helping me out lending me your car after my ban – only for me to write it off – and for being there for me. I will make sure I come over to see you in Spain at least once every couple of months once I've got this football malarkey out of the way.

I would also like to thank David Clayton, my ghostwriter, who rang me out of the blue a few years back to see if I would like to do this autobiography. We didn't know each other from Adam but I am sure he knows more about me now than many of my closest friends and family (until they read this) – thank you pal. It's been a pleasure doing it with you and I think I may owe you a pint or two for doing it!

Tony Heald (my junior school head teacher) for his encouragement and sending me for the Barnsley Schools trials.

Jeff Taylor (Barnsley West End manager) for his support and putting up with me missing all those one-on-one chances.

All my coaches at Barnsley FC during my early days in the

Academy. To Colin Walker (Barnsley FC youth team manager) – this could be a long one – for believing in me at a very early age. Giving me my first YTS and professional contract. Then for putting up with all my shenanigans during my early time as a professional footballer and for basically not giving up on me, which would have been the easy thing to do. I owe a lot to Colin that's for sure, so heartfelt thanks, mate.

Jim Webb (former Barnsley FC physio) for getting me in shape to make my full debut, and as you will see later in the book, covering for me when I had one of my overseas 'misdemeanours'.

To Norman Rimmington (kit man at Barnsley FC) for keeping my feet firmly on the ground. If I was ever shit then Rimmo certainly told me about it.

To Paula (my first girlfriend) for convincing me not to call time on my footballing adventure at a very early age.

To Terry Dolan (former York City manager) for signing me the first time round at York when I was thinking about sacking football off altogether.

To John Askey (then Macclesfield Town manager) for signing me and finally quashing my centre-half career once and for all – and for sticking with me when I couldn't have scored in a brothel with £100 in my pocket.

Peter Taylor (then Hull City manager) for giving me my big

chance back in the Championship which really kick-started my career again.

To Tony Pulis (former Stoke manager now with Middlesbrough) for getting me away from that tanned ball-bag Phil Brown at Hull and for doing my foreword for this book.

Alan Irvine (then Preston North End manager) – the best manager I had in all my career. For signing me at Preston and keeping the faith with me when – once again – I couldn't hit a barn door. And for not taking us on holiday (it will become clear later in the book!)

To my best mate in football, Chris Brown, for letting me live with him while I was splitting up with Clare and for some bloody good times.

To Dr Len Noakes (then at Cardiff City) for helping and supporting me when I hit my lowest point. What a bloody great guy.

To Mark Hudson ('Huds' and ML his wife) for looking after me more than they ever knew they were doing and for being there at one of my lowest points.

To Malky Mackay for hating me that much that I got paid up early at Cardiff City. Just think what it could have been like if he had liked me!

To all the physios I've had over the years – for strapping my ankles every day, which must have been a ball-ache and rubbing my tree trunk legs on a regular basis. And also the chefs at the clubs I've been at – as you can imagine, these have all been very important to me over the years!

To Ady Pennock for signing me at Forest Green when I was struggling for a club and helping me get another five years (plus maybe a bit more) out of my career.

To Jilly Cooper – nice to have one of Britain's best-selling authors write the foreword – and what a lovely woman. I'm already looking forward to the next garden party, Jilly.

To Graham Westley. Some of you might have heard bad things about him and while I didn't agree with his training methods, he was good enough to allow me to go back to York City and go home to Oliver. Much appreciated, pal.

To Jason McGill (the York City chairman) and Gary Mills (then York City manager) for taking a chance on a very old semi-crippled has-been and bringing me back to York City.

To all the players that I have played with over the years. Some have been arseholes, but I've also met some very good people and good friends along the way.

Finally, to all the arsehole managers I have had. Thanks for being such wankers because if you all hadn't been then I don't think there would have been any point writing this book. You all know who you are and by the end of this book, so will everybody else!

To all my mates from Ardsley that I've grown up with and still see regularly to this day. If I've missed anyone out, I'll make sure I don't in the paperback!

Finally, thanks to Will Beedles, Paul Dove, Steve Hanrahan and Simon Monk at Reach Plc for believing in this project, thinking it might make a decent story and making it all happen.

FOREWORD

By Tony Pulis

Jon Parkin was an old fashioned, archetypal centre forward.

He was a throwback to a bygone age and his ties to the community he grew up in are strong in that everyone could associate and connect to him whether they worked down a pit or in a local factory – it didn't matter because in their eyes, he was just the same as they were, and to his eternal credit, he has never acted any differently throughout his career.

There used to be a thread between football and working class people that's largely gone now, but Jon was a genuine thread. He was part of how the game used to be and I found that fantastic to be around.

As a person, he's a wonderful lad, but it's important to remember he was a very good footballer too and I think that maybe gets forgotten sometimes. He had great technical ability and was an absolute handful on his day. He could do stuff that really didn't seem possible for someone of the size, shape or movement that Jon had!

He was never going to fulfil his potential because football has never been everything to Jon – enjoying life and the experiences you have along the way was always more important to him than sacrificing everything for the game, but I found him to be a wonderful lad.

He is without doubt one of the funniest players with the driest sense of humour that I ever had and it was a pleasure to work with him.

He was one of those characters that, no matter whether you were winning, drawing, losing or whatever, he could just come in and lift the place. He used to travel in with Richard Cresswell and he told me a few stories about Jon and had it been anyone else, I'd have gone berserk, but because it was big Jon, I just let it wash by.

I've got many stories about Jon but none that I can really share here!

One that does spring to mind, however, was a time when I had a bit of a go at him for being overweight. I decided to pull Richard Cresswell in who was a great professional and would carshare to training with Jon. I said to him: "I'm going to put the responsibility down to you. You've got to get into Jon about his weight – it's alright me saying it and him nodding his head, but you've got to get into him."

After about six weeks, I went in to see Cres and I said: "What are you doing? It's not working. He hasn't lost an ounce."

Cres said: "Gaffer, we can't get past the first roadside café on the way here! Every time we come in together and he's driving, he just pulls over and gets his bacon, sausage and egg sandwich. It's impossible." I think that was the last time I tried to control Jon's weight.

Jon was – and remains a real old-fashioned character and there aren't enough of them left in football these days, and although there were some times he used to drive me mad, you couldn't ever really be angry with him because he'd just come back with something that would make you smile

He is blunt and straight to the point. What you see is what you get.

I just wish there were a few more Jon Parkins around.

FOREWORD

By Jilly Cooper

Two years ago, I decided to write a novel about football and in an attempt to find a romantic hero and to master the endless complexities of the game, started going to Forest Green Rovers, my lovely local team in Gloucestershire.

On my first visit, I instantly clocked hero material: an extremely handsome, blond hunk of six foot four who was pounding the ball all over.

"Wow! Who's he?" I asked my neighbour in excitement.

"Jon Parkin," came the reply, "known as the Beast. The fans adore him and chant: "Feed the Beast and he will score.""

"What's he like?"

"Hilarious, speaks his mind – party animal, refuses to sacrifice his social life for the sake of football."

Shortly afterwards, I engineered a meeting with Jon Parkin

and found him just as gorgeous, both explaining aspects of the game and regaling me with irreverent stories. Then, a new manager took over and, sadly, Jon left Forest Green for Newport.

He kept in touch, however, and I was thrilled and flattered to be asked to write a foreword to his autobiography: 'Feed The Beast'. Relieved too, because it's embarrassing if a book turns out to be dreadful, but in this case, it is a great read and huge fun. And in case you're planning to give it to your mother for Christmas, it contains extremely strong language.

Born in Barnsley on December 30, 1981, the perfect time of year for a party animal, Jon is the son of proud, loving, wonderfully supportive parents. He adores South Yorkshire and the school mates he grew up with there, makes every effort to get back to the area and feels his book is best read in a broad Yorkshire accent.

Always obsessed with football, he was playing professionally at seventeen. 'Feed The Beast' follows his career over twenty odd years in which he scored 218 goals in 635 games for countless clubs up until the end of the 2017-18 season. So many, he explains modestly, because it took each club a year 'to find out I was shit'. This is disproved, however, by the speed other clubs snapped him up the moment he was free.

But the party animal prevailed, as he confesses. Enjoying

'how's your father' in the afternoon with a girl he'd just met, followed by a vast late lunch of fish and chips was hardly the ideal preparation for his first ever professional evening game.

And so it went on. Endless clubbing until four o'clock in the morning, regularly taking hangovers on to the pitch, being fined for drink driving, continually over-sleeping and arriving late for matches, merrily waving his sponge bag, as his team was coming out of the tunnel. During his first year alone, he was fined four weeks' wages for such misdemeanours.

There are also endless hilarious accounts of holidays abroad so long and riotous, Jon needed another holiday to recover when he came home. One year, returning straight to training, he was so unfit he finished miles behind even the goalkeepers in the first-team jog.

As the years pass, we enjoy reports of stag parties in Benidorm, weddings in Mexico and pre-season trips to train in Tenerife, which saw players climbing out of windows and down fire escapes to get to the party action.

Yet through this time, Jon continued to play brilliant football. For these, he explains, were the years before Twitter and social media and the abstinence forced on players now. Today, they are like laboratory animals, having to eat and drink what the scientific analysers tell them and to keep the FA informed of their whereabouts at all times.

As Jon admits, drinking was acceptable, "Everybody was at it in the past, I just took it to another level."

One loves his honesty and his wild generosity: how when he went off with his future wife to buy a flash car for himself, he bought another one as well for her. While the bonus he received when Stoke City (for whom he was playing) went up to the Premier League, paid for a new house she liked and the entire wedding.

Yet anyone who claims footballers earn too much money to deserve any sympathy will, I feel, change their minds after reading this book. Not just because of the excitement and pleasure they bring to billions of people every week, but because their days of playing only last a few years and because just when everything's going swimmingly, goal drought strikes or, even worse, injury: hamstrings, knees, ligaments, inflicting worse pain than any Spanish Inquisition, putting players out of action for months, even for ever.

In addition, some manager, who admires you as a player and in Jon's case, as the Court Jester, who brightens up the dressing room, is replaced by some little Hitler, who'll promptly put you on the bench for weeks, denting your confidence, and rendering you no longer match fit enough to advertise your skills to other clubs.

Or he'll have you in for a 'quiet word' to tell you he wants to terminate your contract or send you on loan to some club miles away, so you have to find a new home, or exhaust yourself driving back to your family every week.

One is constantly moved throughout the book by Jon's devotion to his son, Oliver, which meant whichever club he moved to, he would always drive miles back every week to spend time with the little boy.

One of the most touching moments is when York City, Jon's club at the time, landed the FA Trophy with Oliver chosen as one of the mascots. Having led his little boy on to the Wembley pitch in front of a crowd of 38,000, Jon scored a winning goal. What a proud memory for father and son.

On balance, over the years Jon has perhaps been too honest and outspoken for his own good. Too many managers opt for 'agreeable' players which means players who always agree with them. In 'Feed the Beast', our hero is gloriously dismissive of the odd chairman, manager or player who caused him grief, but mostly he is fair and generous, and endlessly honest about his own failings.

If he had given up partying, one suspects he'd have been a Premier League star, if not in the England team. But, as one prank follows another, we'd have been deprived of a wonderfully entertaining book.

In a year or two, Jon's playing career may come to a close,

so I hope he moves on to become a creative and charismatic manager. Best of all, I'd like to see him as a summariser on television, perceptively but hilariously lighting up our screens, alongside Lineker, Shearer and Wrighty: a fun-dit rather than a pundit.

KEEPING IT REAL

I t was my first training session at Cardiff City and we had just started some kind of forwards v defenders session. Craig Bellamy, on loan from Man City at the time, passed the ball to me and I controlled it and played it to the guy behind me. Nice and simple, job done.

"Hey! Fuckin' play it back to me next time!"

I looked up and Bellamy had a face like thunder, but I'd never been intimidated throughout my career and I wasn't going to start now. Besides, I was about eight inches taller and four stone heavier so I would have probably shaded the weigh-in.

"Look, pal," I said. "I know you might be used to playing

with Carlos Tevez and Robinho, but I cost one hundred grand. What you see is what you get, mate."

He must have thought, 'What the fuck have we signed?'

In fairness, if he did, he wasn't the first and probably wasn't the last, either – but after 15 clubs, 600-odd games and 200-odd goals from a career spanning more than 20 years and counting, I think I've done okay. I've probably averaged a club for every year I've played, and I've always said that's down to one reason – it usually takes a year to figure out I'm shit and then move me on.

That said, by the end of this book, you might agree that – actually – Parky didn't do too bad, considering. Either that or 'How the fuck has he got away with it for so long…?'

In truth, either opinion is fine by me. I just hope what you are about to read makes you smile every now and then.

Anyway, no bother. Best crack on…

1

RISE OF THE SCROTE

So there I am, still full up from my fish and chips and just hours after a bit of cheeky with the girl I'd met and now I needed to be ready to come on if needed. And I did come on

There might have been a clue as to what was come when I was born just hours before New Year's Eve on December 30, 1981 with most of the world preparing to party.

There were two other portends that day as well with 'Physical' by Olivia Newton-John and 'Don't You Want Me?' by The Human League both in the UK Top 5 – two song titles that would also become recurring, tenuous (and often tedious) threads throughout the career that lay ahead of me. If 'The Wanderer' and 'Show Me The Way To Go Home' had been around then, they would also have fitted nicely considering what lay ahead, but they weren't, so I shan't dwell.

I came into the world at Barnsley General Hospital and for the next 37 years at least, I never liked to drift that far from it if truth be told. Barnsley, for all its faults, is in my blood and I would always try and make sure my football career was spent as close to my hometown as possible. You can take the lad out of Barnsley, but you can't take Barnsley out of the lad.

Before we get going, I'd just like to say that as you read this book, do try and imagine you're hearing it in a broad South Yorkshire accent. If you're going to have Parky in your head for a bit, best speak my lingo if you can.

Reet. On wit'story, as we say round our way.

I was born into a loving, working class family. James, my brother, got here four years earlier than me and in years to come would prove a total bipolar opposite to yours truly – he's academic and an introvert and… well, let's just say I don't fall into either of those categories. We don't look the same, talk the same or act the same. I think my mum and dad might have picked up the wrong baby when they brought me home.

We lived in a three-bedroomed semi-detached and were just your average, normal family. We never went without, but never had a great deal if you get what I mean. We'd holiday in Newquay, Cornwall, every year and Mum worked in a pub and a local supermarket, while Dad worked in the classified car ads at the Barnsley Chronicle.

I went to Lees Hill Infants School to begin with. I never minded school that much, but mainly because I could chat. Every school report would pretty much be the same – 'has the capability but lacks concentration' – in fact, that might have applied to a fair few of my clubs in the future, but we'll deal with that in a bit. I just went to enjoy myself and I made friends there that are still my mates today. In Ardsley, our local village, people don't seem to leave and that's not because they can't; it's just because they don't want to.

On leaving Lees Hill, I attended Ardsley Oaks Junior School, where I was given a load of encouragement by headmaster Tony Heald, who took the school football team, along with Mr Hunt who was also a big influence. Mr Heald would later recommend me for trials with Barnsley Schoolboys and Mr Hunt was the one who explained to my parents what the association with Barnsley Schoolboys and Barnsley FC could mean in the future, so both left a lasting impression.

I suppose I stood out from an early age as I was always taller than most of the other kids. My earliest memory of football was having a kick around with James in our garage when I was maybe four. As I got bigger, invariably at weekends I'd have a bowl of cornflakes, go down the park with my mates and play football all day. By the age of 10, I'd started playing for Barnsley Westend JFC, mostly because my mate Mark Taylor's dad – Jeff – ran them, and my dad did all the admin. My size meant I played in the year above my own age group, though due to league rules, I only trained with the Under-11s to begin with until I actually turned 11 and could play matches.

My coach stuck me up front and – believe it or not – I was pretty quick back then, but I couldn't finish to save my life. I had so many one-on-ones that I lost count and ended up expecting to fuck it up before I actually did. I was shit at them and probably converted one in three or four, but they persevered with me.

Playing for Barnsley Westend, we came up against some strong teams which included Sheffield Wednesday's Young Owls, Sheffield United's Junior Blades, Rotherham United's Junior Millers and many more from the South Yorkshire area. We more than held our own, winning the league in the two years I was with them under coach Jeff Taylor.

We'd train on a pitch next to a local distribution centre, so we could use their floodlights during the winter. In fact, my first memory of being in a pub was a presentation night for wining the Sheffield GT Junior League at the Dial House – a big club/pub in Sheffield – where we collected our trophy in our new tracksuits while Tina Turner was blasting 'Simply The Best' out of the speakers. We thought she'd recorded that just for us! Football and pubs. Hmm. Might have left a lasting impression, that night…

There were trials for Barnsley Schools at some stage during that first year where each club were invited to send their best players and I was sent along with a few more from Westend thanks to Mr Heald. I did okay, too, and ended up being picked to play for them. We'd play other schools within about a 40-mile radius including Chesterfield, Sheffield, Leeds and such like and it was a good grounding for me.

Dad had played football to a decent level though neither him nor my mum pushed me – but they were chuffed when I started playing for Barnsley Schools Under-11s. Dad took me everywhere or else I could never have played, and my parents' support was key at that age to getting things moving. Looking back, it was a pretty smooth transition – almost too smooth when I think about it.

It goes without saying Barnsley were my team and I'd go

and watch them whenever I could, though I'd be playing for Barnsley Schools on Saturdays and West End on Sundays more often than not.

Ashley Ward was probably the first player I wanted to be like and I'd watch from the Brewery Stand at Oakwell where we'd perch on milk crates to see the game. Gary Fleming, Andy Rammell and Brendan O'Connell were players that stuck in my mind from back then and, as a Barnsley lad, it was my dream to play for them. Little did I know representing them wasn't too far away when I was aged 11.

Barnsley Schools were regularly watched by league club scouts and they must have seen something in me because I was invited to the Barnsley FC School of Excellence to represent their Under-13s. That meant the end of my Westend days as I'd be playing on Sundays for Barnsley.

A few lads from Westend had also been picked up by Barnsley and other clubs so we had a farewell trip together to watch England play Brazil at Wembley – a brilliant day. Back then, I had no idea that I'd have three opportunities to play on that hallowed turf in years to come.

Moving to the School of Excellence was a big step up and my first football pay day was just around the corner. Word had got around that I was playing for one of Barnsley FC's junior teams and the local youth club I attended every Tuesday and

Thursday with my mates were having a five-a-side competition against another village youth club. They wanted me to play for them, so I said I'd think about it, but once they offered me two quid to play, the deal was done. We won and, even if I do say so myself, I was well worth that two quid! I was thinking I could get used to being paid to play, though it was a few years before I next earned money for my talents.

I would train Wednesdays with the school of excellence, Fridays would be Barnsley Schoolboys, youth club Tuesdays and Thursdays and play matches Saturday and Sunday. I knocked around with the same group of mates I'd always knocked around with (and still do today) because, as I say, nobody really ever left our village.

Ardsley is not a place many people move to, but it's also a place people are reluctant to leave. It's not particularly picturesque, is an old mining town and is very much old school in many respects, but everyone knows each other and it's a nice place to live. I know I never drifted too far away.

Around that time I'd also started to show a bit of talent in another sport close to every Yorkshireman's heart – cricket. On one particular evening, my parents were close to calling a search party to find out why I'd not come home from school. I eventually rolled in, as kids do, without a care in the world to find Mum and Dad beside themselves thinking I'd been hurt or kidnapped! I'd just been practising in the nets at Darfield Cricket Club and lost track of time, but it paid off as I soon earned the reputation of cracking a few boundaries off when I played with the adults. I was selected for Barnsley Schools cricket team and was in the team that narrowly lost the Lord's Taverners Cricket knock-out final at Harrogate.

My cricket career would never take off fully because of football, but I stayed and kept playing for Darfield when I could – a cracking little club close to my heart. I still turn out when I can. My style of play is to whack the ball to or preferably over the boundary rope. Sometimes it works, sometimes it doesn't, but I mainly just played – and do to this day – for fun. It also led to Mum and Dad loving the game and they still regularly go to Test matches and one-day internationals.

Aged 14 I had to drop the Barnsley Schools and focus on the Barnsley School of Excellence, playing Sheffield Wednesday, Rotherham, Doncaster and other junior sides in our area on a regular basis. I was progressing under coaches Bob Widdowson and Bob Earnshaw and was moved up from Under-15s to Under-16s with them. I'd done well enough to earn a place in the Premier Youth League Under-19s side aged 15 so I knew I was doing something right.

I was playing with 18-year-old YTS lads who were a few years older than me and we'd play our matches at various club training grounds on Saturday mornings. The Under-19s coach Colin Walker had, by this point, wanted me to play some games as a centre-half as obviously I had the physique for it, even at that age. It didn't appeal to me that much, but I didn't want to be seen as some snotty-nosed kid with his head up his own arse, so I didn't question it and just did as he asked.

Danny Wilson was the manager but Barnsley had been relegated from the Premier League the season before and on the first day of pre-season 1998/99, he left for Sheffield Wednesday and John Hendrie took over. Hendrie wasn't that arsed about youth players. We still had a competitive senior squad and were going to have a go at getting back up straight away, which meant there wouldn't be many chances for kids like me to get a sniff.

On the plus side, the Under-19s stayed in the Premier Youth League so we were up against some top sides every week. We were allowed to play three first-year pros aged 19 at that level, so I was up against 18 and 19-year-olds every Saturday morning – lads who were sometimes four years older than me – but still holding my own because I was by then about six foot four.

I remember my first game was against QPR and I was marking Peter Crouch. The ref was Mike Riley and some of the other lads were swearing at him during the game, but it was my first experience of anyone doing that because you weren't allowed to question the ref at junior level. Had my mum and dad not been watching on the sidelines, I think I might have had a go myself. I'd make up for it and more besides in the years to come, but it was a surreal experience at the time.

I played that full season, taking me up to the age of 16. We had about six New Zealand youth internationals in our team because Colin Walker was an ex-New Zealand international in the 1980s. Rory Fallon was among them and he'd go on to have a decent career in England along with David Mulligan who played for a few lower league clubs.

I was hoping I'd be offered a YTS at the end of the season, but instead I was offered a professional contract straight away. I'd only ever wanted to be a footballer, so I was living the dream, though as a 16-year-old, I needed to wait until my 17th birthday in December 1998. Until then, I was on a YTS which paid £50 a week. When I turned 17, my money went up to £250 a week and was backdated to July as a sort of signing-on fee. I got about £50 on top of that for living expenses for board and lodgings, so happy days! I did throw my mum and dad £25 out of that, but the rest was mine to spend.

They always say start as you mean to go on, and looking back, there is little doubt I did exactly that. I'd been included in the reserves squad against Coventry City at Oakwell, but

I thought it was just for the experience. We trained in the morning and got everything ready and cleaned up by 3pm ahead of the game at 7pm. A few of us went into town and I met a girl I knew and ended up having a little bit of how's your father in the afternoon. Afterwards, I was starving so I had fish and chips because I thought there was no way I'd be involved. You're probably ahead of me at this point.

What I'd forgotten was that the subs rule had changed and there were five subs now instead of three and, of course, the reserve team manager told me when I arrived I was on the bench. So, there I am, still full up from my fish and chips and just hours after a bit of cheeky with the girl I'd met and now I needed to be ready to come on if needed. And I did come on.

I was brought on for the start of the second half and at that level, I was up against seasoned pros, some of whom were internationals, as well as Steve Ogrizovic in net. But I thought I'd done okay – probably not as good as I could have done without my afternoon in town – but nothing that had ended my career before it had started.

After that, I began playing here and there for the reserves. I was flitting between centre-back and striker and I was learning more every time I played. I was thinking, 'Fuck me, this is starting to get a bit serious now!'

Other kids around the village seemed to have respect for

me and I suppose when you're at a professional club, some put you on a bit of a pedestal. But none of it was ever going to change me. The bottom line was that I was just a scrote from Barnsley who just happened to be good at football. What could possibly go wrong?

2

ON THE TOWN

She went into the hotel bathroom, closed the door and I heard the shower curtain being pulled back, then I heard, 'What the fuck is that?' That was the conclusion of what we'll now refer to as the the Magaluf Shit Incident

Some girls are attracted to professional footballers, end of story.

That's not exactly a revelation, it's just the way it is, and I suppose you could ask, 'and why not?' Athletic lads with money, it's not rocket science as to why it happens. For me, I suppose girls started to play a part in my life when I started my

YTS when I started going into town with my mates. Barnsley's nightlife was outrageous. One of the bars we used to go in was owned by a Barnsley fan called Paul McNicholas and every drink was £1 to the lads from the club – about £2 cheaper than everyone else. But because it was one of the best bars in town, it meant that some of the coaching staff went in there from time to time as well, which was a problem.

Because of our age, we shouldn't really have been in there at all, so we were constantly looking over our shoulder in case we were spotted. One night, the physio spotted me and told our coach, so I was fined two weeks' wages just before Christmas. It was the first fine of my career and the first of many, but it was well worth it. It was brilliant and I loved being out with the lads and having a beer and it didn't take me long to get a taste for it.

Apart from football, I'd found my vocation. I was making the most of being a footballer, even though I was nowhere near being a footballer at that time. My drink was lager – I wish I could drink something else but I can't and that's probably why I'm the size I am.

I was never a big-time Charlie, and nothing had changed – I was having a ball, though it probably wasn't what I should have been doing at that stage. I used to hate Colin Walker at that time and was always questioning (to myself) why he was telling me to do this, that and the other. I didn't want to be picking up dirty kit or sweeping the stands, I just wanted to play football. I wasn't cocksure exactly, but none of that side of the game ever really meant that much and more often than not, I'd just toss off whatever task I was given.

I'd do the bare minimum and that was it, but Colin was starting to pull his hair out with me. Finally he said: "Look, what job do you want to do? What are you good at that you can do properly?"

I asked him what the easiest task was and he said sweeping the corridor and office, so I told him I'd do that.

The season hadn't gone as well as everyone had hoped it would and John Hendrie was sacked towards the end of the 1998/99 season and first-team coach Eric Winstanley took over as caretaker until the end of the season. Eric was a nasty bastard with kids and was hard, fair but ruthless with it.

All the kids were shit-scared of him because he was old school and had a reputation that had been passed on by the other young pros who'd made it into the first-team squad, but all had a story to tell. As it turned out, Eric was great for me because the moment he took over he told me I was to train with the first-team.

He'd seen enough of me in the reserve games and must have thought I was worth a punt. I knew that, even at that age,

I'd got myself a bit of a name for maybe not doing things the orthodox way, going out too much and wasn't maybe as dedicated as I needed to be but, still, I must have been doing something right.

It was a bit of a shock to the system when he went one better and named me on the bench for the first-team the following Saturday. Eric was a Barnsley lad so whether that helped me out or not I'm not sure, but there I was, 17 and substitute for my hometown club. I was grand as eggs.

We were playing away to Huddersfield Town and winning the game 1-0 with 89 minutes played when Eric told me I was going on to replace Bruce Dyer. I was bricking it if truth be told because all my mates and family were there, plus it was a Yorkshire derby. I don't think I touched the ball and just ran around like a headless chicken for three or four minutes, but we won the game and I was chuffed.

It was like, 'Right. That's it – I'm going out to celebrate!' Obviously, everyone in Barnsley would know who I was now (I thought) and I wanted to push the boat out and I thought I was bound to pull a right cracker as a result – I don't think I did, in fairness, but after an hour or so out I was too far gone to care.

I got another 15 minutes or so in our next game against Watford at Oakwell – a 2-2 draw – so I couldn't really have asked for a better end to the season. I'd broken through and the sky was the limit next year.

Sadly, for me, Eric didn't get the job permanently and Dave Bassett did. He came in in May 1999 and was at a stage in his career where he only wanted proven players because he was basically preparing for retirement. Like John Hendrie before him, he had little interest in the kids and I was back training with the reserves and youth team for the 1999/2000 season and back to square one. I only had two sub appearances all season – one in the League Cup against Stockport County and the other in the FA Cup against Wimbledon, so I hadn't had the chance to kick on much.

In fairness to Bassett, he'd done okay and we made it to the Championship play-off final against Ipswich Town, so all the younger lads who weren't involved and some of the backroom staff travelled down on a separate coach to Wembley. Bear in mind I was a bit of a beer monster now, so when we arrived at Wembley, I went with a few of the lads to a pub where our fans were and sank a few pints and had some decent craic before we watched Barnsley lose 4-2 in front of about 74,000 fans.

It was a shitter because we'd been ahead after just six minutes and thought we might be going back to the Premier League again. We were more than a bit gutted, but as beer softened the pain, I had a brainwave to get a few cans for the journey back. It meant walking in the opposite direction of our coach, but we eventually found an off-licence, got a couple of bags full of cans and headed back to our coach.

We'd been scheduled to leave at 6pm and it was already about half-an-hour past that when we finally turned up and the youth team manager was raging. He took our bags off us, put them on the floor and said: "Get on that fucking bus now!" We sat down, and I was starting to sober up a little bit by then after being pissed for most of the afternoon.

Then I started thinking, 'What the fuck have I just done? Did I really just try and get on an official Barnsley FC coach with two bags full of beer?' I had plenty of time to think on the way home, but when we arrived, that was it for the summer. No meetings, no training, just free for the summer and I forgot all about it.

The reserve team coach didn't. On our return for pre-season, I was fined two weeks' wages for my Wembley shenanigans – about £500 – meaning I'd lost about a month's wages in my first full year as a pro. It wasn't the best of starts for a youngster trying to make his way in the game but I swore I'd never do it again – at least until the next time.

Bassett started the following season and to give me a bit of game time and experience I almost joined a Finnish club called FF Jaro on loan, which I'd have been more than happy to do.

But I was struggling a bit with my groin, which could have been nothing more than growing pains, but I couldn't shake it off and it meant I couldn't go out on loan until I got it sorted.

After trying just about everything, it ended with me having an injection in my pubis bone, which is the most painful thing I've had in my life – Jesus Christ it hurt. Eventually, I ended up having an operation and missed the best part of four months after having corrective surgery that lengthened my adductors to prevent the issue happening again.

While I was out, Bassett left the club in December 2000 with Barnsley nowhere near the promotion pack. Eric Winstanley took over again for a few games and then Nigel Spackman got the job permanently in January 2001.

I knew Nigel from a year or so before when he'd been allowed to train the youth team for a few sessions as part of his coaching badge and for a time, we sort of became his puppets. He knew me from that period and must have liked me, but I was a bit of a mess, physically.

I'd been out recovering from my op all season, played just twice in 18 months and I'd also been out on the piss on a regular basis during my four months recovering. Because of my age, I was able to get away with it, but I didn't need to be told it wasn't the life any footballer should have been leading.

The problem was, I loved a beer and I loved going out. I loved student night on a Wednesday and I was out every Saturday and Sunday, drinking, meeting different girls each time and rolling home pissed at 4am before heading back in to work at about half eight for rehab, more often than not still pissed.

My dad was tearing his hair out, but I was 18 and there was only so much he could do. I just loved it and I was living two lives – one of a professional footballer and the other as an 18-year-old kid without a worry in the world. Drinking was accepted more then and was part of football culture. Everyone was at it. I was just taking it on to another level.

I was back training again and shortly after Nigel took over, he called me into his office and I thought, 'Fuck. What have I done now?' He had brought an incredible physio called Jim Webb in with him from Chelsea and Jim was way ahead of his time, doing stuff not many other physios were doing back then. I sat down and Nigel said: "Right, you're not training for a month. You're going to be with Jim morning and afternoon."

I was thinking, 'Fuck me. Morning and afternoon?'

Nigel must have seen it, too, because he said: "Honestly, you need to do this."

He was right. I did need to do it. He'd obviously thought about me, seen something he liked from his time coaching me and thought about what I needed to do to get into shape, so I thought, 'Fuck it, I'll do it'. So I started the sessions with Jim and I stayed out of the pub for the next month. I was with Jim running and with Jim in the gym, and by the end of the month, I'd lost a stone and a half. I was trim and I was fit.

I went straight into first-team training after that and I could feel it had been well worth it. I also thought I could start going out again now I was a picture of health!

Not long after, we were away to Sheffield United. I had started travelling with the squad with Nigel using me as a centre-back in training, but the team had been announced and I wasn't in the starting line-up. We got on the coach at Oakwell and headed over to Sheffield for the pre-match meal at the hotel. It was a massive game for us and for both sets of fans. After we arrived I realised Chris Morgan, one of our centre-halves, wasn't there so I asked our other regular central defender Steve Chettle where Morgs was.

He said: "Oh, he's ill." We had Brian O'Callaghan who was sort of third choice centre-half and he'd played maybe 25 games under Dave Bassett and seemed the obvious one to drop in. If he did, that would probably mean I was on the bench. I didn't think too much more about it, even though there were one or two butterflies. About half twelve the next day, Nigel Spackman pulled me to one side and told me I was playing. I was a bit gobsmacked and he could see it. "You're playing centre-half with Chets," he said.

I tried to look calm and collected, but inside it was like 'Jesus Christ!'

"You've done everything I've asked of you in training so yeah, you're playing," he added.

I was good mates with Brian O'Callaghan, whose nickname was 'Murph', so I went and told him first. He just said: "Oh, right." He wasn't best pleased – it didn't bode too well for him if I was getting the nod ahead of him. I think he was raging a bit on the inside, but I had other things to sort out, so I went and rang my mum and dad and told them to get to Bramall Lane because I was playing. Then I told my girlfriend at the time, Paula, and she headed over with her mum and sister as well.

Before kick-off, I was shitting myself, I don't mind admitting. I'd be up against Carl Asaba and my nerves had completely gone. As I looked around before the game I just tried to absorb everything. Most importantly, I didn't want to make a cunt of myself. We went back in to get changed and I was physically shaking. During the warm-up, I looked at the stands filling up and it made me even worse. We went back in for a final few words from the gaffer and by that point, my arse had gone, and I was just staring at the floor thinking, 'I don't want to do this, I don't want to do this'.

I kept wondering, 'What if I just say I can't do it?' I was thinking of what I could do to get out of it when Nigel Spackman finished his talk and it was time to go out. I must have been as white as a sheet and I was still considering just turning around and walking back up the tunnel because I couldn't face it. My eyes started to well up and I must have looked like a rabbit in the headlights. What if I just started crying and had 25,000 fans just laughing and pointing at me?

It was all going through my mind, but I was on autopilot by then and just walked out with the lads and looked to my left as I came out and there were about 5,000 Barnsley fans who were right up for it. The Sheffield United fans started singing 'Annie's Song' by John Denver before kick-off and next thing I knew, the game had started.

Asaba was quick and powerful and I knew I had my hands full. So when the ball came to me, I tried to settle myself in with some outrageous pass which, fortunately, went towards our left-back, who managed to get his head on it or else they'd have been in. Then, against the run of play, Martin Bullock puts us 1-0 up and I was thinking as the break approached, 'Actually, I'm doing alright here.' Talk about jinxing yourself.

Moments later a ball was played over the top, Asaba nips in behind me and buries it for 1-1 and just for good measure, it was clearly my fault. Fuck it. I went in waiting for the inevitable bollocking, but Spackman just said I was doing well and that was it. Everyone knew it was my fault but nobody was going to dig me out. I was 18 and making my full debut and all the lads had been there.

We get back at it and after the hour-mark, Neil Shipperley bangs one in the top corner and that turns out to be the winner. A 2-1 win at Sheff U on my debut. I was full of it and I was like King Ping in town later that night with loads of people coming up and saying I'd done well or this, that and the other. I was like a pig in shit. I was up and running, in the limelight and loving it.

I didn't play in the next game because Morgs was okay again, but I was back in for the game against Sheffield Wednesday because we'd been thrashed 4-0 by Preston in between. I was still shitting my pants, but I wasn't as nervous. Wednesday had Gerald Sibon and Gilles De Bilde up front and we ended up losing 2-1 – at least neither of the goals had been my fault!

I made my home debut against Bolton Wanderers and we lost 1-0 before finishing off against Portsmouth on the last day of the season, but we were on the beach by then, losing 3-0.

I was 18, still living at home and was now on £400 per week

plus getting £400 appearance money whenever I played. I had a brand new Corsa, a steady girlfriend and felt like I had the world at my feet. Or some of South Yorkshire to be more exact, which for me was just as good. I had an incredible summer with the lads and went on the piss in Barnsley and Magaluf with a few quid in my pocket.

The guy I was sharing with in Magaluf was a bit prim and proper. He'd gone out and I'd finished getting ready and I suddenly had the urge to take a crap – so I had a shit in the bath, as you do. I pulled the shower curtain across and then headed out for the night.

While I was out, I met a girl and we were walking down the street holding hands in torrential rain. There was that much water on the street that there were these two guys in full wet suits water-plaining down the middle of the road.

Next thing, out of nowhere, one of them wipes her out from behind. She went flying, her purse spilled open and she ended on her back with a cut on her elbow. I helped her up and picked her bag and bits and pieces up. I said: "You've cut your arm, love. My hotel's only five minutes away so we can go there and clean it up if you want?" She said she did, but I was forgetting something.

So, we headed back, went to my room and went in. I lay on the bed and told her she could go and get cleaned up in the bathroom if she wanted and that there was a shower and towels in there. She went in, closed the door and I heard the shower curtain being pulled back, then: "What the fuck is that?!" Then it clicked. She's seen the shit I'd done in the bath. I shouted: "What is it?"

She said: "There's a massive shit in your bath!"

I went: "No way! You're kidding me?"

She said: "You dirty bastard!"

I told her it was the guy who I was rooming with who'd done that. I said: "I went out first – the dirty bastard."

That was the conclusion of what we'll now refer to as the Magaluf Shit Incident.

3

BARNSLEY CHOP

It was classic Parkin. I'd been on the piss for seven weeks during the summer, come back for a week, got a driving ban then gone to Tenerife and ruptured my ankle ligaments while I was pissed and now I was out for half the season as a result

I hated pre-season with a passion.

I'd had a heavy summer in every way imaginable and had drunk too much and eaten plenty, but it had been good. I was so out of shape during the first few sessions that even the goalkeepers beat me at the running. I struggled through it and gradually worked my way back towards fitness.

Then one day I had a massive row with Paula and went into town for a few pints. I decided to drive into town and get a taxi back and get my head down.

I got absolutely twatted. Like a moron, I decided I'd drive back instead of getting a cab and managed to get about a mile from home when I saw the blue flashing lights in my rear-view mirror. I knew I was fucked. I was so drunk I'd even pissed myself in the car, so I pulled over and after failing a breathalyser, I was taken to the station where I was tested again. Somehow, I was only just over the limit – fuck knows how, but I was over and that was the bottom line – then they gave me my keys and allowed me to drive home!

All the way back I was thinking about how to tell my parents and then the club. I'd say telling mum and dad was the harder of the two, but as there was no way of covering something like this up, I had to come clean. I waited a few days until the letter arrived giving me the court date, got my parents together and gave my dad the letter. He looked at it and shook his head. My mum was just perplexed – they weren't angry, just disappointed, I think.

I then took the letter into work, went to Nigel Spackman's office and said: "Gaffer, I need you to have a look at this." He read it and said: "Right. Well, you've got yourself in a bit of shit here, Parky."

Then he must have clocked the time I was arrested – 4.30am which probably pissed him off even more.

"What the fuck are you doing out at 4.30 in the morning during pre-season?"

I said I'd had an argument with my missus and just lost my head, but I think the fact he'd shown faith in me, invested time getting me fit and given me a chance disappointed him the most. I'd played in four of the last six games of last season and I'd repaid him by being arrested for drink-driving. Whichever way you looked at it, it wasn't good.

He told me to sort it, but he had a resigned look on his face.

A week or so later, I was in court for sentencing and the local press had sent some guy who spotted me, just as I was on my way out of the hearing. The following Friday, the headline on the local paper was 'Barnsley's Jon Parkin caught drink-driving' and suddenly everyone in town knew about it. The car was locked away in the garage as I served my 12-month ban and there wasn't much else I could do other than keep my head down and work hard.

We flew out to Playa de las Americas in Tenerife for the final part of our pre-season training and because of what had just happened, I hadn't even been sure if I would be included or not – but I was and I was relieved. I roomed with Murph who was one year older than me and after the first evening, we found out most of the other lads were sneaking out at night and going clubbing on the strip.

They were climbing out of windows and fire escapes and after a few nights, me and Murph thought 'fuck it' and got dressed to go out for a few beers. We got to the top of the fire escape and I suddenly had second thoughts. I knew if I got caught on the back of drink-driving, I'd be kicked out of the club for good. I was already clinging on by the skin of my teeth, so I told Murph I wasn't going and he said "fair enough" and we went back to the room.

Some of the lads were stinking of booze the next morning, but I managed to keep my nose clean for once. We had a game against Tenerife the day before we flew home and I played half the game and did okay. Later that evening, we set off for a bar in town where there was a sponsor event we had to attend before being allowed out for the rest of the night. The logical thing, having just been banned and severely pissing off my manager, would be to have a beer back at the hotel and get an early night.

Not a chance.

I went out with the lads, hammered it and had a proper binge as I made up for lost time. The next morning, we had a bit of a warm-down planned before the flight back to England. My alarm went off, but the room was spinning like a top and I was still in a bit of a state. I tried to stand up, but my ankle gave way and I fell back down on the bed. I tried putting weight on it, but it was fucked – a bit like me. I must have sprained it on the night out, but fuck knows how. I couldn't remember a thing and the beer must have numbed the pain.

I was already in the last chance saloon with Nigel Spackman, so I managed to hobble down to training, but I was in a right old pickle. We had a few gentle jogs and I managed to somehow get through it. It was sort of accepted by the coaches that we were all worse for wear and that was that.

We packed, went to the airport and flew back home, but I was in agony with the beer now fully worn off. My ankle doubled in size during the flight and I knew I was in massive trouble. Before we headed home, the gaffer told me we had a friendly in a couple of days' time and that I was playing. I just nodded.

There was no way I was going to make it for that game or any game for the next month or so, but I just needed to think of something that could keep me out of the shit.

I pulled the physio Jim Webb before we left the airport and told him what had really happened. Jim liked a drink too and was sort of sympathetic to my plight, so he told me to call him the following morning and tell him I'd got up, tripped over my alarm clock wire and twisted my ankle.

So the following morning, I phoned him: "Jim, you'll never believe what's happened..."

"Go on," he said.

"I've just got out of bed and I've twisted my ankle falling over my alarm clock wire."

He just went: "Right-oh. Come in and see me in an hour."

I got dressed and headed in where Jim was waiting for me. He only had to look at it to tell it was a bad sprain. "Fucking hell, Parky! It's massive." He shook his head and sighed before letting the manager know. No more was said of it, but I was ruled out for maybe three months with ankle ligament damage.

It was classic Parkin. I'd been on the piss for seven weeks during the summer, come back for a week, got a driving ban then gone to Tenerife and ruptured my ankle ligaments while I was pissed and now I was out for half the season as a result. What a balloon I was.

Worse still, we were really struggling and by the middle of October, the gaffer was sacked. I'm not saying me playing might have saved him, but I owed him a lot more than I'd given him for the trust and belief he'd shown in me. Who knows? I might have helped turn a few defeats into draws and a few draws into wins, but we'll never know, and he was gone.

I'd not long been back in training but was making good progress. Glyn Hodges took over for a few games as caretaker and I was given an unexpected recall. We were playing Newcastle United in the League Cup and Glyn threw me in at centre-half. It was a relief just to be playing football again, but I looked at the Newcastle front four of Alan Shearer, Craig Bellamy, Laurent Robert and Nolberto Solano and thought maybe I could have waited for another game to come back!

It was a team packed with internationals and, predictably, we hardly saw the ball. They were like the Red Arrows and I hurt my neck twisting it this way and that trying to keep up with them, but I did okay and didn't embarrass myself. They scored in the 79th minute to win it 1-0 but being up against a team like that and doing okay made me wonder if I maybe could hold my own after all.

I played in the next two games as well and I'd have been happy enough if Hodges had got the job, but in mid-November the club went for Rochdale manager Steve Parkin instead. He'd done well at Mansfield Town and then Rochdale and had just turned 34 – and it didn't take long to make his mind up to get shot of me. He knew about my drink-driving and my recent injury record and had probably made his mind up on me before he even walked through the door.

I think he wanted to put his stamp on the club because there were one or two big characters at Barnsley back then. He had Little Man Syndrome and walked around the place like he was carrying two carpets under his arms, but the more experienced lads weren't having him, and it was like 'Fuck off you knobhead, we'll be here longer than you.' He wouldn't even last a year, but that wouldn't matter because he would outlast me.

I steadily built up my fitness, played a few reserve games and Steve Parkin calls me into his office. He told me he wanted me to go on loan to Hartlepool for a month and I thought the move made sense. I could get a few games under my belt, get my match sharpness back and come back and challenge for a first-team spot, so I said it was fine by me.

Because I was banned, my dad would drive me the two hours from our house to Hartlepool on a Sunday and I'd stay at a little bed and breakfast outside of town in the coastal village of Seaton Carew. Adam Boyd would pick me up from the B&B and drop me back. The only issue was the manager – Chris Turner – wasn't playing me as agreed. I had nine minutes off the bench and that was it.

They were doing quite well at the time, but it was a complete waste of time for me. I didn't want to rock the boat, so when I was told Hartlepool wanted to keep me for another month, I just went along with it. I remember going out to a nightclub in Newcastle while I was there and a few of the Newcastle lads were in. I was at the bar and Alan Shearer came up.

"You alright mate?" he said. "How are you doing?" I looked behind me to see if it was me he was talking to. "I played against you up at Barnsley a few weeks back."

I knew he had. I also knew it was Alan Shearer. He asked me what I was doing in Newcastle and I told him I was on loan at Hartlepool and he nodded and said: "All the best anyway, mate." It was decent of him. He was the most expensive footballer in the country, a Newcastle United legend and he was making time to speak with a teenager nobody had really heard of outside of Barnsley.

Around that time, my mate Chris Harris was training to be a British Gas engineer in Newcastle and we'd occasionally travel back to Barnsley together. I was having a shit time at Hartlepool and I'd been left out of the squad again for the next game, so I was happy to see Chris and travel home knowing I had the weekend off.

On the way, the Hartlepool physio called me and said I needed to get in for training the following morning at half ten. I told him I would struggle to get back for that time as I was back in Barnsley overnight, so he just told me not to worry about it. I thought that was the end of it.

My logic was that if I was training Saturday morning, I wouldn't be playing for Hartlepool Saturday afternoon. I wasn't travelling 100 miles to get hypothermia in the stand in the middle of January. Hartlepool in the winter isn't pleasurable, believe me.

I travelled back up with my dad on the Sunday evening to my B&B, had a kip and was woken by my mobile next to my bed. It was Steve Parkin. I wondered what he wanted at that time, so I answered it. "Alright gaffer, what's up?"

He said: "Who the fuck do you think you are? Why didn't you go to the game at Hartlepool on Saturday?"

I was wide awake now. I told him I wasn't involved, they hadn't been playing me and I had trouble getting back for morning training. Plus, the physio said it wasn't an issue.

He said: "You are a disgrace. Twenty years old and not turning up for a game? You are a fucking cunt."

I said: "Gaffer, I wasn't supposed to be playing. I was training."

"You were on the fucking bench! Right, well you can fuck off! You're fined two weeks' wages and you can forget it here, pal. And Hartlepool don't want you any more, so you can forget them as well."

He hung up. I admit, my first thought was 'not another two weeks' fine'. All that for nine fucking minutes of football.

I was in the shit again but this time I didn't think I'd really done anything wrong. I called my dad and he said he'd come and pick me up later. I was in the hotel alone and I called up

Paula and told her I'd had enough. I told her I was done, and I meant it. I couldn't be arsed being treated like and talked to like a twat and I just wanted out. She said not to make any rash decisions and to get home where we'd have a chat about it, but in between my dad picked me up and I explained what had happened and told him the same.

By this time, I'd had an agent for a couple of years, a guy called Tim Webb from Worcester who had taken me on his books when I was aged 17 and would stay with me my whole career. I phoned him, and he just said. "Look Jon, you're just 18, don't pack it in now. You're just starting out and you don't know what's around the corner."

I managed to cool down a bit and went back to Barnsley to train, knowing I was just kicking shit, but I had to go through the motions.

I had other things on my mind at that time, too. My best mate from school – and still is today – Jamie Ravenhill, had been in a tragic accident. He was involved in a motorbike crash with his cousin. They were on a dirt trail when they'd been in a head-on collision with a motorbike going the opposite way.

His cousin Brett was in intensive care for six weeks and the kid on the other bike was killed. Jamie broke both his arms and was in a bit of a mess. His cousin ended up having his leg amputated below the knee.

When Jamie came home, I decided I needed to look after him, so I turned up on his doorstep with my bags and told him I was moving in for a bit. "I suppose I'm gonna have to wipe your arse for you as well, aren't I?" He said: "No thanks! You won't have to go that far, mate." He was living with his mum, stepdad and brother, but they were out and about a lot so I thought I'd be able to help out in the afternoons after training.

Training at Barnsley was doing my head in until, at last, Tim called to tell me York City wanted me to go on loan for a month. They were second bottom of the Football League, but they said I'd definitely play games, so I said: "Okay, I'll do it."

What a year it had been. Banned from driving, my ankle injury, Spackman sacked, Parkin coming in, all the shit at Hartlepool and Jamie's crash – it felt like I'd run down a dozen black cats. It was by now the start of February and I hadn't played a full league match since the previous May. I needed a fresh start and I needed to get away from Barnsley. I'd played about 15 games since making my debut three years earlier, had stalled and gone into reverse.

To get to York, I'd get a taxi from Jamie's to a place where Peter Duffield met me, and he'd give us a lift to York up the A1. Duffs was a decent lower league player and, unlike me, he looked after himself, so it only took a few journeys before he was tearing his hair out as I asked him to pull over so I could get sausage rolls and Coke on the way in. On the way back, I'd have fish and chips!

I had a couple of training sessions with York, got to know the lads a bit and Terry Dolan – the manager at York – was true to his word and I was in the starting line up away to Southend United.

I was unfit and blowing out of my arse, but I could see light at the end of the tunnel when the clock said 80 minutes played and I knew it'd soon be over. That's when Graham Potter (now manager of Swansea City) lofted a cross into the box and I nodded it back across goal and into the opposite corner for what turned out to be the winning goal.

It wasn't just the winner, it my first professional goal and I'd done it as a striker, but I couldn't celebrate because my legs were that stiff I could barely move.

That goal gave me the bug for the game back a bit. Our next game was against Halifax Town and I played the first half up front and the second in defence in a 1-1 draw. I was still going out on the piss three nights a week and driving Duffs mad, but I was doing okay and having a bit of an impact at York. I was gutted when the month's loan was coming to an end and it was a relief when Terry Dolan took me to one side and asked if I'd stay for another month. I think I took him aback a bit when I asked if he could go one better and sign me up for good.

He said: "Why would you want to come here permanently?" I told him I'd do it in a heartbeat and then phoned my agent to help make sure it happened. He came back to me and said York were offering a two-and-a-half-year deal, which was perfect. The deal was done pretty quickly and I left Barnsley and signed for York City on a free transfer.

Steve Parkin couldn't wait to get rid of me and the feeling was completely mutual. I was on £700 a week, was guaranteed regular games and even had a bit more beer money.

4

BANGED UP ABROAD – AND HOME

"Unprofessional? We've got one fucking football, a size five that's out of shape, no cones and one team running about in skins in the middle of winter on a shite training pitch and you're calling me unprofessional? You can fuck off, mate!"

I'd gone from wanting to jack it all in to joining a club that wanted me and a club I wanted to play for. It was tough leaving Barnsley because they were my hometown team and in an ideal world, that's where I would have stayed, but there had been no future for me under Steve Parkin.

York was commutable, which was important as I was still

banned from driving and there were always one or two lads that could give me a lift into training. Bootham Crescent was an old stadium with a good atmosphere but the club was struggling and I needed to contribute to help them stay up.

We were second bottom when I arrived, and we ended the season closer to the play-offs than the relegation zone in mid-table, so I suppose the gamble paid off for everyone. I hadn't set the world on fire with just two goals in 18 games but had played my part and survival had been the most important thing.

I was looking forward to enjoying myself in the summer so when my mate's mum said she was going to pay for a holiday to Zante and asked if I would I like to go with them, I think I'd answered her before she finished the sentence. She booked it for her son Craig Marsh, me and Jamie, who was still recovering from his bike accident but had come on leaps and bounds. On the day we were leaving, Jamie found out his passport had expired so it was just Craig and me who headed out, with Jamie flying out with another lad a few days later when he'd sorted his passport.

I stayed a week, but when it was time to fly back, I wasn't ready to go home. So me and Jamie decided to stay on a bit longer and booked the room on for another week. We were staying in a Club 18-30 hotel and it was absolute chaos, but we were loving it. Opposite our hotel there was another hotel next to a bit of wasteland. We'd spied crates of lager at the back of it and decided to half-inch some one evening. It was pitch black and we snuck around the back, grabbed a crate and started to leave. That's when the guard dog we hadn't clocked started to go nuts. A moment later, a torch came on and two guys from the hotel came out the back, spotted us leaving with the crate and started chasing us.

We ran back to our hotel and went to our room, not knowing if they were behind us or not. The banging on the door a few moments later suggested they had been! We blanked the banging and then after about five minutes everything went quiet and we thought we might have got away with it.

Then we saw blue flashing lights outside our hotel bedroom door. They started banging on our door with their coshes so Marshy hid under the sheets while I stayed on the toilet, naked – that was the best thing I could think of to avoid getting a bit of a beating. I said to Jamie he should go and answer it and finally, he did, jumping back into bed as soon as he had opened the door as we waited for the inevitable.

The police came in and were ranting and raving at us in Greek. Eventually, they demanded our passports and said: "9am, tomorrow – police station!"

It was starting to sink in that we might be in a bit of bother.

We turned up at 9 but didn't have a clue what they were saying to us. I was thinking about what happened in the movie 'Midnight Express', but instead of being thrown in jail, we were released without our passports, not knowing what was going to happen next. A few hours later a police car stopped as we were walking down the street and told us to get in.

We went back to the station and I thought maybe we would be thrown in prison – but the two guys from the hotel agreed that if we paid for the crate we'd stolen that would be the end of it. So we did, got our passports back and decided stealing booze in Greece probably wasn't the smartest idea.

By the end of our second week, neither of us wanted to leave, so we binned the flights and stayed. It was like, 'Fuck it. Why not?' I had nothing to get home for, even though I'd only brought a week's worth of clothes.

I had no cash so had to get my dad to wire some money over and stayed for a third week. Every night we were out partying and drinking till the early hours. When I eventually got home, I felt I needed a holiday.

That said, I went out the Friday night we got back plus Saturday and Sunday, too. I'd been out for about 24 nights in a row and on the Sunday, the other lads had just about had enough and decided to go home – but I wasn't ready, and I got a taxi into town on my own to carry on. An hour or so later,

I was stood in a bar on my own having a pint and I suddenly thought, 'What am I doing?' I'd been out on the lash every night for close to a month and I still hadn't had enough. I began to wonder if I might have a bit of a problem because although I was enjoying myself, this was above and beyond normal boozing.

I drank up and headed home, wondering what I was doing and where I was heading. I sort of gave myself a bit of a shake and decided I wouldn't go out again that summer, save for the odd pint here and there.

I hadn't trained for even an hour in the summer so when I turned up for pre-season training and the other lads were asking each other how much they'd been doing while they were off, they couldn't believe I'd done absolutely nothing. We had to do six laps of the training ground to get us going and I was blowing out of my arse after about two. I dug in, tried my hardest and eventually I started to build up my fitness and burn off my summer excesses.

We went to Durham in pre-season for a four-day training camp and on the final night, four of us decided to go out on the piss and headed for the bright lights of Durham city centre. We found a bar we liked and stayed there until about 1.30am when the York assistant manager Ady Shaw sent a text to Mike Basham saying, 'Where the fuck are you?'

He didn't hang around and got off straight away but the rest of us carried on, thinking we would just have another hour. Durham was dead and everywhere was shut so we headed back and next morning after breakfast Terry Dolan lined us up like a firing squad. He said: "Which of you cunts were out last night? Step forward now…"

I thought, any minute now, he'll get out a machine gun and the Durham Four will be no more.

I was wondering whether he knew who had been out and just wanted to see whether we'd come clean or not but I thought, 'What the fuck?' and stepped forward. The others did, too.

Dolan said: "You set of cunts. I'll deal with you on Monday."

We had the weekend to stew on everything and then on Monday afternoon we had to attend a meeting with the chairman. We went to the boardroom for the inevitable bollocking and the chairman said: "You four are a fucking disgrace." I was thinking, 'I've been here before…'

But I wasn't expecting what came next. He said: "I want to sack you. I want to sack you because that's the right thing to do… but I can't because of PFA rules…"

After having our arses kicked, we were fined one week's wages and told we were all doing community service as a punishment at various old people's homes around York, starting after training the next day. Mine was a place that didn't seem that arsed whether I was there or not so when I got there I said: "Hi, I'm Jon Parkin from Barnsley and I'm here to do a few hours' community service," and the lady on reception just said: "Erm, okay, just go and mingle with the residents."

I went and sat down for a while and then played dominoes for about an hour with some old boy and that was it I never went back. I thought, 'Fuck it, they're not bothered whether I'm there or not, so what's the point?' And that was my community service done.

But my brush with the authorities was far from over. One day, on the way to training, I got a call out of the blue. It turned out to be a policeman from Barnsley who had come into the club to give the lads a talk on handling ourselves around town and crowd safety and what not. I knew him, he knew me and then he says: "What were you doing Saturday night?"

I couldn't think of anything in particular – but started getting that old familiar sinking feeling, so I said: "Nowt, why?"

He said: "Right, well you're in a spot of bother..."

It turned out that something had happened on the previous Saturday. There was a group of girls we regularly went out with. They lived together and occasionally, after a night out, we went back to theirs to carry on the partying. I knew I'd not done anything wrong, so I wasn't that worried. That was until the policeman said: "You've been reported for flashing."

What the fuck? Flashing? I had done some daft things, but this was a new one even for me.

He continued: "About 7am last Sunday morning somebody matching your description opened the curtains at the address concerned and shouted to a passing woman 'excuse me love' and started waving their old man at her."

I said: "Okay, okay, what do I need to do?" He told me I needed to go to the station that afternoon and so I agreed I'd come along after training. I called my mate who had been out that night and was the same build as me, tall with short brown hair. He was now the prime suspect for DI Parkin. I said: "What have you been doing, then? This might have slipped your mind but by any chance did you happen to flash at some woman walking her dog on Sunday morning?"

I heard a resigned sign at the other end. He said: "Yeah, I did."

Bingo. I told him that I had to go in and see the police about it as they thought it was me. He said: "Oh shit!" – and I immediately knew why. He was training to be a teacher and that would be the end of his vocation if he was convicted for flashing so I told him that so long as I could take the rap without any consequence, I'd do it. That's what friends are for, as the song goes.

I went to the police station and was interviewed about the

incident and after they asked what had happened and pressed the recording machine, I said: "I woke up at seven, opened the curtains and, as I did, a woman was passing walking her dog, so I said 'excuse me love' and then started waggling my old man about."

It was so cringeworthy that I almost couldn't carry it through. They took notes then asked me to sign a paper explaining they were giving me a caution for flashing. As we left the interview room, I said: "I hope you know that wasn't me, it was my mate, but he's training to be a teacher." The policeman said not to worry as it was all done now.

The thing was, when I was considering jacking football in, I'd enrolled on a course to be a nursery nurse and had been training at Barnsley College. It was a 20-hours-a-week course with a placement at the end and I really enjoyed it. It might be the last thing you'd imagine I'd want to do, but I loved it and thought I might return to it when I finished playing.

But I'd need a CRB check before I could do the placement and when it was submitted I was on pins waiting to see if I'd be thrown off the course for being a flasher. Thankfully, it never showed up, but I told my mate that if it had, I'd have to retract my confession! As it turned out, injury meant I never completed my college course as I had needed to go in for rehab every day and couldn't get the 20 hours a week needed, so that was that. It was a shame because, as I say, I loved it and it would have been a good qualification to have under my belt. Incidentally, my mate did qualify as a teacher so it all turned out as well as it could, I suppose.

My first full season with York should have ended in promotion. We missed out on the League Two play-offs by four points and the main reason for that was that we'd gone into administration from December until March. We won just four of the next 15 games and fell away as a result, just missing out on the play-offs when we probably shouldn't have.

A lot of the lads couldn't pay their mortgages during that time and were going into games wondering what was going to happen. Anyone who thinks that doesn't matter at League Two level hasn't got a clue. I was fine – I was back at my mum and dad's, so I didn't have any major concerns, house to lose or kids to feed. I was on about £800 a week with bonuses so I had money anyway and my parents' backing if I needed it. I'd also split up with Paula by that time so every penny I had, apart from a bit of board and lodgings, was mine.

I'd made 44 appearances all told, scoring 11 goals. I was

happy with that because I'd played some games as a striker and some as centre-back, so I knew I'd made a decent contribution. Yet I couldn't help wondering if I was under-achieving. I was a Championship player playing two tiers down and felt I should have more to show, but in some ways, I'd had to start over and York helped me love football again. I'd had my first full season behind me and things were back on track.

Despite a big improvement on the pitch and all the administration shit we'd had to deal with, Terry Dolan got the sack at the end of the season and club captain Chris Brass took over as player-manager. At 27, he was the youngest manager in the Football League. He knew what I was like on and off the pitch and I was in and out of the team under him, which was disappointing as it felt like I was going backwards again.

We were struggling as well. Then, after Christmas, things went a bit pear-shaped. It was around January and we were training on a pitch that was no more than a mud bath. The youth team were playing that day so when we arrived there was no equipment for us to train with. No balls, no bibs – nothing. We had one old misshapen ball and without bibs, one team had to play in skins in the middle of winter – and, of course, I ended up as a skin.

It was a bit of a shambles and during the session, I picked up a clump of mud and slapped it on the back of one of my team-mates. It was just a bit of fun and I did it a couple of times, if nothing else to highlight how bizarre the whole session was for a set of professional footballers. Brass had started playing me regularly around that time but when the team was named for our next game the following day he told me I was sub.

I went into his office to find out why I'd been dropped again, and he said to me: "Yesterday at training you were throwing mud – it was unprofessional."

Steam started blowing out of my ears. I said: "Unprofessional? We've got one fucking football, a size five that's out of shape, no cones and one side running about in skins in the middle of winter on a shite training pitch and you're calling me unprofessional? You can fuck off, mate!"

I stormed out, grabbed my washbag and went home. I know I shouldn't have but I was so pissed off I just wanted to get away before I said or did something I'd regret even more. I was supposed to be on the bench, but I couldn't be arsed.

The following Tuesday, Brass pulled me in and told me I'd been out of order which, in fairness, I had, but I wasn't about to back down. I told him he was out of order for dropping me in the first place. The next game, I was sub again, but this time I took it on the chin and just got on with it. Then, the next game, I was sub again, but came on and did alright, even though we got battered 4-1 at home by Lincoln City.

I wondered what my future was at York given the past week or so – and that's when I got a call from my agent telling me Macclesfield Town were interested in signing me. With York's financial situation, I knew they wanted me off the wage bill, so I said, yeah – I was definitely interested.

They were similar to where York had been when I joined them in that they were second-bottom of League Two, but I knew it would be a pain in the arse to get to Macclesfield from Barnsley across the Pennines. It was probably no more than 30 miles, but there was no fast route there, so although I was keen to move on, I had to think about the travelling involved.

I had to factor in going to training dog-rough on a Monday morning – as I normally did – and the same on a Thursday after Sunday and Wednesday nights out, but when the contract offer came through, it was better money than I was on at York, so I thought, 'Yeah, I'll take it.'

Macc had offered me an 18-month deal, the manager was John Askey and on February 20, 2004, I signed for Macclesfield Town on a free transfer. Askey told me all he wanted me to do was score goals and keep Macclesfield in the league – no pressure then! I don't know if he knew I had also played at the back, but from then on, I played as a striker all the time – my days as a part-time centre-half were over.

The Macc fans were great with me, but even if I'd been shite, they could see I was trying and they seemed to take to me straight away. I think with any football fan, if they can see you're trying, that goes a long way to keeping them off your back.

As it turned out, I started badly in terms of goals and couldn't hit a barn door. After avoiding the drop, it wasn't long before the club decided to bring the more experienced Brian Horton in as manager with Askey dropping to be his assistant. That was a bit of a strange one but he accepted it as he'd already been with the club about 20 years.

I'd scored no goals in my last eight York games before I'd left and with just one in my first 12 matches for Macc I'd managed a princely total of one goal in 20 games combined! The irony was, that one goal came in a 2-0 win at York at a time when whichever side lost, it was going to be a mountain to climb to stay in League Two. It was a real six-pointer with only seven games left. Macclesfield were on the up while York were dropping like a stone and in deep shit.

I scored on 19 minutes and another former York player, Graham Potter, scored the second and York couldn't respond. I'd enjoyed my time at York, so I didn't over-celebrate, even though me and Brassy had sort of parted company under a cloud and it was my first goal in more than five months.

That win, plus three more in our last six matches (two of

which I missed with a knock) meant we ended up seven points above the relegation zone – York City were relegated out of the Football League, but I still had unfinished business with them and our paths would cross again in the years to come.

5

MACC LAD

> *I'd never remember to wash my kit and I'd turn up with damp gear that had been in the back of my car stinking. Plus I'd be rough as fuck after nights out on Wednesdays and Sundays. It was no wonder I pushed all the wrong buttons. I wasn't a model pro*

Summer – have fun and enjoy life. Pre-season – struggle and look a bit of a cunt for a few weeks. That was my mantra and even if it felt like Groundhog Day, I had no plans to change my ways. The summer weeks belonged to me, I'd earned them, and I would pay the price in July. Nothing had changed by the start of the 2004/05 season. That said, I hadn't had a mad summer for once. I'd had a lads' holiday but I'd also met a girl who would later become my wife.

Her name was Clare and she was a psychology student from Barnsley. Fittingly, we met at the Heaven and Hell nightclub in Barnsley and we'd known each other since school, but she was in the year below and I'd never really had much to do with her. As it happened, we got along really well and started dating through the summer months and that helped me calm down a bit, though I was still out on the lash every Wednesday and Sunday night.

We kicked off away to Leyton Orient on a red-hot August afternoon in East London and I scored twice in a 3-1 win at Brisbane Road. I'd equalled last season's magnificent tally in one match and was hopeful that this might be a decent year for me. I managed six in my first five games and, as it turned out, it was one of my best seasons yet. I'd hit the ground running and I didn't stop. By Christmas, I'd scored 14 goals, was playing as well as I'd ever played, plus we were doing alright in the league.

In fact, we were in with a sniff of promotion going into spring and towards the end of March we had a Friday night game away to Swansea City at Vetch Field. I was being marked by Izzy Iriekpen, their centre-half, but he seemed hell-bent on winding me up. Every time we went up for a header he smashed me, whether it was in the face, chest or ribs.

He must have caught me with his elbow four or five times and, eventually, I started losing it. We went up for another header and he smashed me again and knocked the ball into touch. I was raging by that stage and as the ball went out of play, it hit the advertising board and came back to me. I smashed it, sweet as a nut, towards where our left-back was jogging to take the throw-in — only he missed it and it went into the crowd and hit a kid plum in the face.

I was gutted as I'd just lashed out without thinking, but of course the game went on. As it did I glanced over to where the kid was and I could see the St John Ambulance in the crowd. I just thought, 'Fuck, what have I done here?'

The crowd were giving me pelters and I was feeling like a right twat so when the half-time whistle went a few minutes later, I went over to see if the kid was alright. I leaned over the wall and asked if he was okay and his mum said: "Just fuck off!" I thought I best go in for the break instead.

The game carried on and Iriekpen was still smashing me at every opportunity, the crowd were giving me shit and I had the kid on my mind still, so when the opportunity for payback came, I was about to blow. He was about to clear the ball on the wing and I thought I'd give him a bit of his own medicine and slid in at speed, but he saw it coming and ended up on top of me. As he went to get up, he grabbed my balls, so I stretched out a leg and volleyed him full in the face.

Everyone missed it apart from the linesman behind us – time

to say my goodbyes. I was sent off with about 10 minutes to go and, though we were 2-0 down, Horton slaughtered me at full-time. He shouted: "You've let us down! We're trying to get in the play-offs and you've let everyone down."

He was right, too. We didn't win any of the three games I was suspended for and so slipped out of the play-off spots. Not my best moment in a Macclesfield Town shirt. We'd won just one of our previous eight games and couldn't have timed a shite run any worse, though the most damaging loss was against leaders Southend United. I hit a free-kick against the post and David Morley put it the rebound on 26 minutes to put us ahead, but we ended up losing 2-1 with almost the last kick of the game.

For whatever reason, we'd lost our momentum and needed a point on the final day against third-bottom Rushden & Diamonds at Moss Rose. We were edgy and they were the better team with our keeper Alan Fettis playing out of his skin. But we kept at it and when Kevin McIntyre spotted me at the far post, he swung the ball in and I volleyed into the opposite corner with an hour played. We clung on to win 1-0.

So, including the Swansea defeat, we'd taken nine points from our last 27 and missed out on automatic promotion by five points. Horton had been right. The Swansea game had really cost us but I felt the loss against Southend was even worse. I felt responsible in some ways because the bad run had started at Vetch Field and we just couldn't shake it off. We'd made the play offs but it felt like an anti-climax and were up against a Lincoln City side who had only beaten us a few weeks before.

We lost the first leg at Sincil Bank 1-0 and then went behind at Moss Rose before ending up 1-1 and losing 2-1 on aggregate. It was disappointing but we'd come a long way inside a year and I'd managed 26 goals in 51 appearances which, for a 23 year old, was bound to catch people's attention, though nobody came in with a firm offer I knew of.

Besides, I was enjoying playing for Macc and I went into my third season with them feeling settled and happy with life. I enjoyed the summer with Clare, I'd bought my first house in Barnsley and she'd moved in with me.

I came back for pre-season in the usual state but worked through it and was looking forward to building on last season. We were going to give it a good go and our first pre-season friendly with Manchester City at Moss Rose in mid-July would tell us a bit about where we were at as a team. I knew it was a good chance to make an impression against a Premier League side and Moss Rose was packed, mostly with City fans.

It started well, too. On three minutes the ball came into the box and I nipped in between Sylvain Distin and David

Sommeil and put us 1-0 up. I was flying, full of beans and was giving the City defence a few problems. Then on 10 minutes I went up for a header with Richard Dunne but as we landed, he fell on my leg from the side and my knee felt like it just caved in. I knew it wasn't good straight away and our physio, Paul Lake, came on and helped me hobble to the side.

I wanted to carry on because we were playing City but I lasted maybe another three minutes before I had to come off again. Lakey thought I'd done something serious but said we'd have to wait until I had a scan before we knew how bad it was.

The scan showed I had a grade 2 to 2.5 medial ligament injury – a three would have meant an operation, but it still meant I was basically fucked. I was given two casts to wear which covered all my leg, with hinge joints restricting my movement. It was a bit like wearing a suit of armour but it meant I wouldn't play again for more than three months. I had rehab, but I soon got bored and frustrated and needed to fill my time with something other than physiotherapy.

It was around that time I started betting, something I'd never really taken much interest in. It soon got out of hand. Horses, betting shop machines and whatever took my fancy – it didn't take me long to rack up about twenty grand of debt. I kept it from Clare and it wasn't that hard to because we had separate bank accounts, but I still had the mortgage and bills to pay. Eventually, I had to turn to my mum and dad for help, even though I was earning about £1,400 a week. I was struggling badly, so I was grateful when they bailed me out by borrowing £20,000 against their house, with me paying them back monthly until we were square.

The cast finally came off and though I did some work with Lakey, I wasn't really match fit or in good shape to begin with. By the end of October, I was back in the team. I'd scored four in 11 games since coming back but we had only won six out of our first 26 games by Christmas.

I liked Brian Horton, but I used to drive him around the bend. Getting to Macclesfield wasn't the easiest with the traffic issues I had, and I must have been late for training two or three times a week – and one thing the gaffer couldn't abide was lads getting in late. It was his pet hate, and if you add the fact that I'd also never remember to wash my kit and I'd turn up with damp gear that had been in the back of my car stinking – plus I'd be rough as fuck after nights out Wednesdays and Sundays – it was no wonder I pushed all the wrong buttons. I wasn't a model pro by any stretch of the imagination.

It was costing me a few quid, too – it was £10 for the first late, £20 for the second and so on and it was hitting my pocket. Finally, I said to Horton: "Gaffer, if I score on Saturday will you let me off with the fines?" He said okay and while I was at Macc, I saved myself a few quid by scoring at the weekend.

On Boxing Day we were at home to Stockport County who were bottom of the table and managed by Chris Turner, who hadn't played me during my loan spell at Hartlepool – you could say he'd started the cycle of shit I'd ended up in at Barnsley, so I sort of owed him one.

I'd not gone mad over Christmas – I never did – so I felt good when I got to Moss Rose. The lads started coming in and one of them, our centre-back Dave Morley, was blind, stinking drunk. Of all the games to come in pissed for!

I loved a beer as much as anyone but always tried to be sensible before a game. One time I didn't was when I was at York and we were away to Torquay. I was rough. I played centre-half and after 20 minutes, we were 3-0 down and all three goals were my fault. I got dragged off on 34 minutes and I've never been so relieved in my life. After that, I thought, 'never again'.

So Dave Morley is in a right state and we were thinking, 'Our centre-half is still drunk – what chance have we got?' There were nearly 5,000 inside Moss Rose, plus it was a local derby, so we were up for it, but knew we might struggle at the back. As it was, they had a man sent off on 17 minutes and me and Clyde Wijnhard scored two just before the break. We went on to win 6-0, so Morley got away with it.

We beat Chester in our next game and then were away to Wycombe on January 2. Brian Horton said we were fine to have a New Year's Eve drink but nothing silly as we'd be playing 48 hours later.

"No worries, gaffer..."

I went to a dinner dance with Clare in Sheffield and got absolutely twatted.

We were training at 12 the next day and then travelling to Wycombe but when I arrived, all the other lads were the same. Nothing silly had turned into something daft. We were all hanging out of our arses and the session wasn't the best. Wycombe were second and had a decent team, but despite the condition of the lads, we went 3-0 up inside 13 minutes – it was nuts. Three shots on target, three goals.

Wycombe got a dodgy penalty just before half-time and with 15 minutes to go, had pulled it around and led 4-3. I volleyed home for 4-4 on 76 and five minutes after, I headed what would be the winner. A 5-4 win – we ended up getting away with that one!

It was around this time that Brian Horton gave me a

nickname that would stick with me for the rest of my career. A reporter must have asked him about the goals I'd scored, and he just said: "Yeah, Jon's a bit of a beast, isn't he?" and it kind of stuck from there on. I know Wycombe's Adebayo Akinfenwa would also be known as The Beast in years to come, but I'd like to think I got there first!

I'd scored nine in 15, we were halfway through the 2005/06 season and I knew there were one or two clubs looking at me and if the goals kept going in, sooner or later I might get a chance to go back up a league or two. I didn't have to wait long. Horton called me into his office just after we'd been beaten 3-1 by Boston United and told me Macc had received a bid for me.

My agent Tim Webb had called to keep me in the loop so I already knew someone was in for me. The gaffer told me it was Hull City who had come in – but then said: "We're not selling you."

I'd just turned 24 and I'd scored about 35 goals in 70 games for Macc and was one of the most prolific strikers of the lower leagues so I knew my stock had never been higher. Hull is about an hour from Barnsley and they were in the Championship so I wanted to go. They'd offered about £250,000 with another £150,000 in add-ons, but Horton said: "I think we can get more money for you."

I said: "What do you mean you're not selling me? I've come here on a free, done brilliant for you and this is my chance to jump up and kick on."

Horton shook his head and, though I could see his point and it was fairly cheap given my record, something just flipped in my head and said. "Right, I'm not playing Saturday."

He said: "What do you mean?"

I said: "Honestly, my back's just gone and I'm not going to be able to play. In fact, I don't think I'll be able to play again for the rest of the season because it's getting worse with every minute. It's really sore. If I were you, I'd cash in on me while you've still got the chance."

I still don't know why I did it, but there was no turning back. So here's Brian Horton, former manager of Manchester City with more than a thousand games in management and he's got this cocky little shit Jon Parkin in front of him telling him he wasn't going to play for him again. He must have thought I was a right cunt. But I knew I had to do it.

Horton let out a deep sigh said: "Right, then. You'd better have a word with the chairman."

I said: "Alright. Come on then."

I don't think Horton had expected me to say that. We stomped across the pitch to see Rob Bickerton and when we got there I said: "Hello Mr Chairman. The gaffer says you've had an offer from Hull City for me and I want to go – and if you stop me going, I'm telling you now, I'll not play another game for you this season because my back's just gone and it's really sore."

Everyone knew what was going on. The chairman shook his head and I said: "Right, I'll leave it with you both," and walked out of his office. As I was walking down the main stand at Macc, I was thinking, 'What did I just do?' Yet I knew I had to do it for the sake of my career.

I'd not long been in my car, heading back home, when Tim, my agent, called telling me I needed to head for Sheffield, where I had a medical for Hull City. "Brilliant," I said. "Absolutely brilliant." My back was starting to feel a lot better already.

I turned up a few hours later for my medical and Championship medicals are a lot stricter than the ones in League Two. It went on for a bit and when everything had been completed, they told me I'd failed! The knee I'd injured when Richard Dunne fell on me was the problem and the doctor told the guys from Hull that he didn't think it was strong enough, so was failing me.

I started to think about what I'd done at Macc and the bridges I'd burnt as I left. I'd been a right prick and now it looked as though it was going to come back and haunt me.

Hull had put a two-and-a-half-year contract on the table and Peter Taylor was the manager at the time. I'd already played 15 games that season and been scoring goals so to my mind, I'd proved my knee was okay.

I got my agent to ring the Hull chairman, Adam Pearson. He told him in view of the medical, we'd be prepared to accept an 18-month deal instead of 30 months and then we'd need to take it from there if everything went well. It meant less security for me but given what I'd told Macc, I needed to move on and was desperate to take the chance.

Thank fuck Hull agreed those terms. I signed the deal and was officially a Hull City player. It had taken me 157 games, five years and a lot of hard work to get back to the Championship, but it had been worth the effort. All I had to do now was make sure I didn't screw things up.

6

TO HULL AND BACK

Phil Parkinson had done well
with Colchester United and he
was the manager Hull turned to
for the 2006/07 season. I
immediately had a few concerns
when I saw him at pre-season
training with a clipboard

I'd gone from being paid £1,300 per week to about three grand a week plus £500 per appearance and £500 per goal – so if I played and scored, I'd be roughly quadrupling what I'd been on at Macc. It was also a lot easier for me to get to Hull from Barnsley.

If I'm honest, I felt a bit intimidated when I first arrived at Hull and I was questioning whether I'd be able to do it at Championship level. It was a massive step up and obviously I'd be playing with better players. They had Ian Ashbee, Damien Delaney, Ryan France and Nick Barmby in the squad and they also signed Darryl Duffy at the same time as me.

At my first training session I was a bit apprehensive, but things went okay and, on the Saturday, I was named in the starting line-up against Crystal Palace. I was nervous as fuck – not as bad as I'd been on my Barnsley debut, but I just wasn't sure whether I was good enough for that level.

There were almost 20,000 inside the KC Stadium and I got a decent reception when my name was read out before kick-off – even though they were most likely thinking, 'Who the fuck is this? We're second-bottom of the Championship and we've signed a League Two striker?' If they were, I was only thinking the same thing.

We started badly and were 2-0 down with 20 minutes or so played, with Leon Court putting one in his own net to double Palace's lead. But a minute after Leon's howler, I got in behind the Palace defence and scored. I wanted to go nuts but as we were losing it was a bit of a muted celebration.

We ended up losing 2-1, but on my drive home, I started to come around to thinking that I might be able to do it in the Championship after all. I'd been up against the experienced

Darren Ward but I'd held my own and, in truth, it hadn't been as difficult as I'd imagined.

In fact, things got even better and we started picking up points. We won at Stoke and Luton and six games into my time with Hull I'd scored four goals – a few of them were important ones, too. We'd started to climb the table and by April, we probably needed one or two wins from our last six games to be safe.

We had a home game with Leeds United and the KC was packed. I think it was a noon kick off and a red hot day on Humberside. I'd travelled down with Sam Collins, Ryan France and Matt Duke and halfway to Hull I realised I'd left my boots in the back of my car in Barnsley. We were too far gone to turn back and while the others thought it was funny, I just thought I was a complete dickhead. I had to borrow Kevin Ellison's Predators which weren't the most comfortable, but they just about did the job.

It was a massive game for us and a bit of a derby. As the game started we were doing well against a decent Leeds side when one of the lads crossed it in, their defender Sean Gregan got his head half on it and it fell to me on the corner of the six-yard box. I cushioned the ball on my chest and volleyed it from an angle past Neil Sullivan and into the net. Our fans went wild and so did I as I set off to celebrate – only to see the linesman's flag raised. For fuck's sake – he'd thought it had come off a Hull head to me when it was Gregan so there was no way I could be offside. To this day, I'm still raging about it if truth be told. The magnitude of the game, against Leeds in front of a full house, it would have been incredible, but it wasn't to be and it was chalked off.

Just before half-time I had a half-chance from close range and Sullivan managed to push it around the post. I went in at the break thinking it was going to be one of those days, but as the game wore on, we were well on top. Leeds didn't look like scoring, so we knew we had a real chance.

On 76 minutes, Stuart Green put in a looping cross towards the back stick, I jumped up against Gary Kelly and headed it down. Sullivan dived across but could only parry it up into the top corner of the net. The KC went nuts and I charged off to the side going crazy, ending with a knee slide and, this time, no linesman's flag. That was the winner, we were safe, and it was happy days all round.

On the Monday, the chairman Adam Pearson phoned Tim and said: "Look, he's got another year after this, but we want to extend it back to the original two-and-half years we originally offered." It was exactly what I'd hoped would happen and meant I had another two years at Hull.

I signed the new deal and thought, 'Fuck it – I'll treat myself to a new car.' I'd never had what you'd class as a footballer's car before, so I went to the local BMW dealership with Clare and picked out a new soft top but she saw one she liked as well, and I ended up buying her one, too. It was my own fault for taking her along, I suppose! Hull ended up surviving by 10 points, so I went away for the summer feeling contented and relaxed. For once, things had gone according to plan.

During the close season, Crystal Palace came in for manager Peter Taylor, which was a bit of a shitter. I half wondered whether he might come back and take me with him – I'd got on well with PT and enjoyed playing for him, but with it being London, I don't think it would have worked out. Too far from Barnsley. As it happened, nothing materialised anyway.

It wasn't all sweetness and light, though. I was still gambling too much around this time and now I was earning a lot more, my bets were bigger too. I think Clare had half an idea that something was going on, but probably wasn't certain enough to challenge me about it. We'd moved into a bigger house as well as I learned to enjoy being a Championship footballer, but my time on Humberside was about to take a wrong turn.

Phil Parkinson had done well with Colchester United and he was the manager Hull turned to for the 2006/07 season. I immediately had a few concerns when I saw him at pre-season training with a clipboard – plus he'd not signed me, and he had probably heard about my previous and my close-season habits. I'd enjoyed the summer break as I always did and had a great holiday. As I say, after 10 months' hard slog, the summer is for resting and enjoying yourself, which I always made sure I did.

Parkinson brought in Stuart Hales as the fitness coach and had Frank Barlow as his assistant. Frank was always as good as gold with me but Hales was an absolute aresehole in my opinion. We did the various tests you do on the first day back, and also had our fat counts taken – mine was always high and always will be – but as usual, I just thought I'd work my way back to fitness gradually.

We went on our first pre-season run and I was at the back – not for the first time in my life – but to Phil Parkinson, this was a bit of an issue. He either thought I was tossing it off, or just massively unfit. After the first week back, we went to Spain on a pre-season training camp. It started okay and I was happy to follow Parkinson's target regarding my fat count. He was the gaffer and if he thought I needed to be fitter, fair enough. It meant I got a free ticket into Fat Camp.

Keith Andrews had a fat count of 14 per cent and he needed to be 12 per cent – yet he was the fittest lad at the club and always at the front when we went on runs, so he was pissed off when he was also put into Fat Camp. He wanted to know why as he'd never had to do that before. So he challenged Parkinson, who told him it was simply because his fat count was too high. For Keith, that wasn't good enough and it was a case of, 'Fuck this, I'm off.' And he left.

We returned home after a week training in the sun and started our pre season programme against North Ferriby, with Parkinson looking to give every player some game time and gradually build our fitness up. During the match, I had a bang on my big toe and had to come off. I knew it was bad and it turned out I'd broken it. While I could run without pain, it hurt when I kicked the ball. For my rehab, I had to be in at 8am every day with Stuart Hales, doing weights and running on the treadmill, which was fair enough.

By the start of the season, Parkinson asked me if I was fit to play and I said I could so long as something was done for my toe. They told me I could have an injection that would numb it and after asking if that would be okay and being reassured, I told the doc to get on with it. We started with a 2-0 loss at West Brom and though I didn't feel that much pain during the game, the next day it was so bad I could hardly walk. That was how things were for the first few weeks. Injection, play, next day crippled, but I scored two in a 3-2 home defeat to Barnsley after we'd been two goals up so it was worth it.

Stuart Hales had come in with all these different ideas and been giving us caffeine supplements and Red Bulls to take before a game. As a player, you trust the professionals and give it a go. They know best, right?

During the Barnsley match, Ryan France had been smashed in the face and come off with concussion. I went to hospital afterwards to pick him up, as we travelled in together. I'd had the caffeine supplements Hales had given me, but I felt totally wired up. I've never taken speed, but I was thinking that it probably felt similar to how I was feeling now.

I called Ryan up and he said he'd been checked over and would be down soon, but all the time I could feel my stomach rumbling and I knew what was coming – I was going to shit myself. I got out of the car to go to the hospital toilet, but just two steps along and I knew I'd never make it.

I had to squat down by my car, still in my Hull City tracksuit, and let the floodgates open. There was shit everywhere. Luckily, I had a golf towel in the back of the car so I used that to wipe my arse before tossing it away for some unfortunate fucker to come across. I got back in the car and started sweating and shaking.

My stomach started rumbling again and I had just managed to get out and drop my kecks before having another massive shit by the car. When I'd finished, I had to half hitch my pants up and then find the shit-covered golf towel and use it again. If I'd been on CCTV I'd have been fucked.

That night, I didn't sleep a wink and by 5am, I was still wide awake. It wasn't right but I put it down to a stomach bug to begin with. I scored another in our next match against Derby and then we played Ipswich Town away. I was still training with the fitness coach because of my toe and fat count and two days before the game, I came in at 8am as normal and he had me doing power squats on my legs – something I'd never done before.

By the time we played Ipswich, I couldn't feel my legs after about 15 minutes in. My muscles were hurting that much that I could hardly move and as I chased a ball in front of our dugout, I pointed at Hales and said to Parkinson: "Keep him away from me! He's fucking useless!"

I had a bit of a tantrum, I admit, but I couldn't believe a trained fitness specialist would do leg weights exercises a few days before a match. I managed to see the game out, fuck knows how, and we drew 0-0.

On the Monday morning, Parkinson pulled me in his office. "What was all that about on Saturday?" he asked.

I told him: "Your fitness coach has had me doing powerlifting weights two days before a game and I couldn't move after 15 minutes at Ipswich. He's useless."

Parkinson said: "Yeah, well that's what you should be doing."

I told him I'd never done them before and that he could see what the end result was, but he told me if I kept doing them, I'd soon get used to them. I said: "I don't want to fucking get used to them! You can see that it affected me. And all that shit he's been giving us before a game, I'm not taking it any more. Fuck it."

Parkinson sighed and looked at me. "Do you know how lucky you are to be a footballer?"

I was, by this time, confident I could hold my own at Championship level and asked him what he meant by that.

He said: "Do you realise how many millions of people there are who want to play football?"

I told him he was talking nonsense and he asked me what I meant. I said: "I'm a professional footballer because I've worked my bollocks off to be a professional footballer. I've been given the tools but I worked my balls off to get to where I am."

He said: "Yeah well…" but I cut him off and told him I didn't give a fuck.

I hadn't finished, either. "So you're telling me a brain surgeon is lucky to be brain surgeon? What's he had to do to get where he is? Work his bollocks off from probably the age of nine until he's nearly 30 is what he had to do, so while he was given the tools to do what he does, he's grafted his balls off to make it happen."

Parkinson said that football was different and I said: "Is it fuck! If you're saying I'm lucky to be a footballer, it's bullshit. I've worked my balls off to get here, so let's agree to disagree. Just keep that fitness coach away from me. I want nowt to do with him."

And that's where I left it. I played in our next two games, and while I don't know if Parkinson thought I was just a troublemaker or an absolute arsehole – or somewhere in between – the fact is I was then dropped to the bench for our next game away to Birmingham City.

I was mostly pissed off because I didn't think any of this had been my doing and when I came on against Birmingham after 78 minutes, we were 2-1 down and I was still raging. I was booked for my first challenge and on 90 minutes, I went up for a header with Radhi Jaidi but led with my foot to make sure I didn't get smashed, caught him and was sent off.

My head was up my arse by this point and I walked off the pitch towards the tunnel, but when I got there, there were two bouncers outside with their arms folded.

"You can't come in here, mate."

For a minute I thought they had a nightclub inside the ground. I said: "Give me a break, pal. I've just been sent off."

"No, you can't come in here."

Cheers pal. I now had to walk back in front of all the Birmingham fans who were giving me dog's abuse and finally got to the changing rooms with the game by now finished. Parkinson gave me a bit of a dressing down and I could sense by now he wanted rid of me.

He'd brought in some of his own players including Nicky Forster, who we knew was his pal. Although we were a bit dubious about him initially, he turned out to be a great lad. Michael Bridges was also brought in and he would score the winner in our midweek win over Leicester that I was banned for, but Forster was injured in that game and I started our live Friday night game with Sheffield Wednesday.

I was still having injections in my toe and wasn't fit because I couldn't train properly. We brought Danny Mills on loan and he gave a penalty away after four minutes against Wednesday. We came back into it and after 11 minutes I headed home the equaliser and six minutes after that, the ball came over my shoulder and I span and volleyed it past the keeper to make it 2-1 with only 17 minutes played.

That ended up the final score and I'd scored two goals live

on Sky Sports – happy days! Maybe not for Phil Parkinson, though, who knew he'd now have to play me, at least for the next few games.

HAD MY PHIL

> *Pulis asked me to fill in on the left of midfield. Let's just say I wasn't a natural left winger! I ran up and down like a man possessed and probably worked a two-foot deep channel down that side of the pitch, with my influence on the game absolutely zero*

Part way through the 2006/07 season, Phil Parkinson fetched Phil Brown in as a coach and, to start with, we got on alright. Brown was a decent coach – but you could see he was desperate to get the job and probably couldn't wait to see the back of Parkinson.

After my goals against Sheffield Wednesday, I had a decent

run back in the side, but couldn't buy a goal and we were struggling again. I'd gone eight games without scoring before I bagged one in a 3-2 win away to Southend United, but I think by that stage Parkinson had had enough of me and I was then dropped for the next four or five games.

Of the games I missed, we lost 5-1 to Parkinson's old club Colchester United and 4-2 at home to Southampton and that was enough for the board and he was sacked. Was I bothered? I didn't mind Parkinson and, in fairness, he gave me a lot of games, even if I probably wasn't his cup of tea as a player.

Inevitably, Phil Brown was handed a caretaker manager role and then got the job permanently shortly after a decent run of results took us out of the relegation zone. I thought I might be alright under Brown but, fuck me, he goes and brings in Steve Parkin as his No.2 not long after. After the shit I'd had with him at Barnsley, I knew it wasn't going to be a particularly happy reunion.

I'd established myself in the dressing room as one of the characters at the club and felt settled at Hull so I wasn't looking to move on and I made sure Steve Parkin knew I wasn't having him.

At Parkin's first training session we were on the Astro at Hull University and I was just blanking him throughout. He was trying to make conversation with me but I wasn't having any of it. At the end of the session, Phil Brown says: "Parky, come over here with me a minute," and we went and sat in his car.

He said: "Obviously I've brought in Steve Parkin as my assistant and I know you worked with him at Barnsley, so what do you think?"

I've never been one to hold my tongue, especially if I feel I'm right, so I said: "He's an absolute cunt."

Brown asked what I meant, so I told him what had happened at Barnsley and he just said: "Oh, okay. Well he's my assistant now so see how you get on."

It was a bit of a cringeworthy situation if I'm honest because Parkin was new to the club and knew that I had influence in the dressing room, so he was going over the top trying to talk to me and be chatty. I'd dismiss him with one-word answers and while I was never rude to him, he would have known I wasn't having him, and so reported it back to Brown.

I was playing but was in and out of the team so when Tim called me up in March and asked if I wanted to go Stoke on a month's loan, I was well up for it. He told me he'd spoken to Hull, who were fine with it, and that Stoke manager Tony Pulis wanted me to go there. Hull were second bottom of the Championship and Stoke were sixth and pushing for the Premier League, so it wasn't a hard decision.

I was full of flu at the time the deal was agreed and hadn't trained for three days but Pulis wanted me to play on the Saturday. I went over to Stoke, trained on Friday and made my debut against Southampton.

After my first game for Stoke, Phil Brown had done a radio interview after Hull's match the same day and a few of my mates had heard it.

The interviewer had asked him why he'd let me join Stoke on loan while Hull were second bottom and he'd said: "I need players who are committed to the football club. I want people who are willing to work hard for this football club, so that's why I've let him go to Stoke."

I hadn't heard it myself, but my mates had, and they'd called me to tell me. Basically, he'd hung me out to dry and I was raging. If he didn't want me, fair enough, but to bring my character into question was out of order and I wasn't having it. I called him the following Monday and asked him to explain his comments about me.

He asked what I meant, and I said: "Well, I've had two people call me up over the weekend saying that you'd said I wasn't willing to work hard for the football club and wasn't committed – that's why you let me join Stoke. Are you saying I'm not committed and don't want to work hard?"

He started backing down: "No, no I didn't say that…"

I said: "Well two people have told me you did. So, any fans

going home and listening to that will think I'm an absolute cunt and that I'm just tossing it off."

He denied it again and said he'd go and get a recording of the interview and get back to me. I told him to do that. I never heard back from him.

Back at Stoke, we'd taken four points out of nine, but I hadn't scored in any of my first three games, so I was dropped for the next match, but back for Leicester when I finally broke my duck in a 4-2 win. I was back on the bench against West Brom and we started well and were 1-0 up after 14 minutes through Ricardo Fuller. A few minutes later Mamady Sidibe had to come off. We then scored twice in two minutes to go 3-0 up after 22 minutes with me getting the third.

After the break, Pulis changed a few things around. We were three up and he asked me to fill in on the left of midfield for a while. Let's just say I wasn't a natural left winger! I ran up and down like a man possessed and probably worked a two-foot deep channel down that side of the pitch, with my influence on the game absolutely zero. I was subbed on 65 minutes. Striker and centre-back? Yes. Left winger? Definitely not.

I was fine though – I'd played about 50 minutes, scored a goal which meant I got my goal bonus and appearance fee as well as showing my versatility! I started in the next game on Easter Monday and scored again as we beat Palace 2-1. Stoke were heading for the play-offs and I'd started to come out of myself a bit and was enjoying the craic with the lads.

Then I got a call from Tim who said Hull wanted me back.

After the Brown radio interview I thought my time there was over. Phil Brown never spoke to me once throughout my month with Stoke and yet suddenly he wants me back? I'd scored three goals in my last three games for Stoke and I was raging. Not only did I not want to go and play for him again, Stoke had a real chance of going up and if I played my part, it might lead to a permanent deal – but with Stoke a Premier League team.

There was nothing I could do about it. I had a couple of days off and headed back to Hull on the Thursday, driving towards training with steam coming out of my ears. I went in, got changed and went out for training. Just before we started, I stomped over to Brown and said: "I want a word with you."

All jovial, he said: "Parky, how you doing?"

I said: "Don't fucking 'Parky, how you doing?' with me. Why did you never get back to me? You're out of order, what you said about me."

There was nobody in earshot and while I wasn't exactly disrespectful, it obviously wasn't the way you're meant to speak to your manager. He denied it again and said he hadn't said that.

I told him: "Well, the fact you've never got back to me is clarification enough that you did say it and that's what you think about me. It's absolute bollocks."

He started stuttering and asked me what I wanted to do about it then. I said: "You've called me back haven't you? Listen, you're a fucking cunt and you'll always be a cunt. If you pick me to play, I'll play for those lads over there. I'm not fucking playing for you. Just do what you want."

He'd brought me back, but I played 11 minutes off the bench against Colchester and then another 20 minutes off the bench against Stoke, then he dropped me for the last two games. Hull were safe by that point and Stoke had fallen away a bit so it looked like a pointless exercise for all concerned.

I'd made my mind up I couldn't play for Brown again and I needed a move away, quickly. In the meantime, Brown brought Brian Horton in, who I knew well from Macclesfield Town. Stoke had come back in and wanted to sign me and Tony Pulis phoned me a few times over the summer to make sure I was going there, so I knew he really wanted me.

I had an end-of-season meeting with Brown, as all the players did, and he asked me what I thought of Stoke's bid.

I said: "Just accept it and let me go. You're a fucking arsehole and I'm not playing for you again."

I saw Brian Horton while I was there and he said: "Parky, I want you to stay." I told him I wasn't playing for Brown again. I said Brown and Parkin were arseholes and that he'd find out soon enough.'

Stoke's offer was a three-year contract and they were willing to pay Hull £275,000 rising to £450,000 based on appearances, goals and promotion. It was perfect. I was finally free of Phil Brown and I was looking forward to the next chapter with Tony Pulis, a manager who really wanted me to play for him and where, as the song goes, things could only get better...

8

STOKE AND MIRRORS

I burst through the door and into the library. Nobody else but the librarian was there. I asked if I could borrow the fax machine and I'd explain why later. It was 4.55pm and I had five minutes to receive the forms, sign them and fax them back

I still liked a pint and still liked to gamble.

I think my reputation was still intact and while I wasn't going mad drinking or gambling, Tony Pulis knew that if I stayed in Barnsley, there was no way I was going to change my ways. As a condition of signing for him, he told me I'd need to move to Stoke or at least somewhere nearer the club.

He told me to get away from my pals in Barnsley and I said: "Yeah, no bother. I'll do that."

I had no intention of moving down.

Stoke had wanted to just take my contract over from Hull, same terms, same everything, but I said I wanted a better deal than I'd been on because of this, that and the other. They were okay, tweaked it a little and after we'd got it sorted, I signed.

As always, I struggled after returning from the summer break, but Tony was aware of what I was like. He was very old school and tough, but he was fair. He was massive on fitness, but I managed to get through my first pre-season okay.

The first-choice pairing up front was generally Ricardo Fuller and Mamady Sidibe just behind him. Sidibe worked hard while Ricardo was lazy – but then he'd do something outrageous and win you the game. He'd do it often enough to keep his place in the side. To be fair, he did what he did well.

We headed out to Austria for pre-season and had one very high-profile friendly while we were out there that everyone was desperate to play in. Real Madrid had wanted the hotel we'd booked but had left it too late, so they offered to play us in a friendly if we swapped hotels.

I very nearly fucked it up for myself though, while almost killing our first-choice keeper Steve Simonsen in what has come to be known as 'The Golf Buggy Incident' – at least

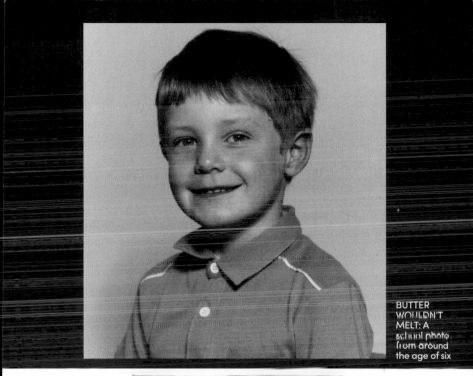

CLOSE FAMILY: On holiday with Mum, Dad and older brother James

FIRST TEAM PICTURE: Our Ardsley Oaks junior school team – I'm third from left on the back row

TROPHY HUNTERS: Barnsley Westend U13s. That's me on the back row, fourth from the right

DREAM JOB: My first official Barnsley photo

BRUSHING OFF BELLERS: In Barnsley action against future team-mate Craig Bellamy

CITY BOY: A loan spell at York City went well, so I signed for them

MACC ATTACK: My goals at Macclesfield Town really got me noticed

TIGER TRAIL: Here I am banging in a penalty against Middlesbrough in January 2007 after Hull City gave me the opportunity to play Championship football

GOING UP: With Stoke City I was part of the squad that earned promotion to the Premier League in 2008 – and I got to work with manager Tony Pulis

UP FOR GRABS: During a big cup tie against Liverpool this grappling session with Jamie Carragher cost us an equaliser!
Right: Against Javier Mascherano

BANGING THE BRUM: Smashing home from close range for Preston against Birmingham City in December 2008

WELSH WORRIES: Cardiff City got so fed up of me scoring against them, they signed me in 2011. Things soon turned sour though and I was looking for an escape route

DON AND DUSTED: My time at Doncaster Rovers was brief but fun, thanks to manager Dean Saunders and his unorthodox training sessions

SPOT KING: I managed a few goals in my loan spell at Scunthorpe United, including this penalty against Charlton in 2012

PROMOTION PARTY: Two years at Fleetwood Town included a League Two play-off semi-final win over York City, leading to a Wembley win in the final against Burton Albion

FOREST FAN: I didn't know where Forest Green was initially, but when I found it I grew to love it and stayed for two years

PIECE OF SILVER: After a brief stint with Newport County I began my second spell with York City where we won the FA Trophy at Wembley in 2017

WEMBLEY WITH MY BOY: Oliver, my son, with me after Forest Green's National League play-off final loss to Grimsby in 2016, then on a happier occasion as I scored and won with York in 2017

DAD AND LAD: A tender moment as I get a hug from Oliver after my 200th career goal

GARDEN PARTY: Me with two of my favourite ladies – Lucy and Jilly Cooper

GOOD TIMES: I enjoy friendship, football and the odd pint – and things haven't worked out too badly!

that's what they called it when it appeared in The Sun! We had an afternoon off a couple of days before the Madrid friendly and there was a golf course quite close to our hotel so a few of us decided to hire some clubs and go out for a round. We hired a buggy and I partnered with Simmo and started the round. We played a couple of holes before we came up to one where the tee was at the bottom of a fairly steep, gravel hill.

I told Simmo I was going to go for it in the buggy, so we drove to the top of the hill and I decided I was going to spin it – I'd always wanted to be a boy racer, so this was my moment.

I span the wheel on the buggy and it tipped to one side. I knew I had to bail out quickly, so I leapt out and splattered on the floor while the buggy span before rolling twice and eventually it came to a standstill. Simmo was still inside. I thought I'd killed him.

I tentatively said: "Simmo? Are you alright?"

He appeared, looking dazed.

"What the fuck are you doing?" he asked. I looked at my shin and it was bleeding and had bits of gravel embedded in. He was okay, thank fuck, but I was bleeding everywhere.

The golf buggy was a write-off. The window was smashed, the roof was dented and the bars at the front were all bent. I just said: "I think I've fucked the buggy up."

We managed to roll it back upright and chugged our way

back to the club shop and explained we'd had an accident. The guy told us it would need sorting, which I accepted, and we headed back to the hotel to see our physio, Dave Watson.

I said: "Dave, we've had a golf buggy incident."

Not for the first time in my life, I heard the immortal words: "For fuck's sake, Parky." The leg was badly grazed with gravel still in it, but there was no way I was going to miss the game. He cleaned my leg up and removed the gravel and said he'd explain what had happened.

I was bandaged up and I had my shin pads over that and my sock and though it was painful, I was okay for the bench. They had Sergio Ramos, Pepe and Raul playing and when I came on for the second half, I was being marked by Fabio Cannavaro, capped 136 times by Italy.

I tried a 40-yard chip that skimmed the bar. It would have been nice if it had gone in, but they knocked it around in their sleep and won 2-0. It had been a piece of piss for them.

I asked Cannavaro after the game if I could have his shirt and he nodded, took it off and handed it to me. As I walked away I felt a tap on my shoulder and he pointed at my shirt. I said: "You want this?"

He just nodded and I was thinking, 'What the fuck for? To wipe your dog down after a walk?'

I handed it over, we shook hands and that was it. I still have his shirt, framed in my house. I bet my quadruple XL Stoke shirt with 'Parkin' on has got pride of place in his house, too.

I'd winced my way through, but I was glad I did as I'd have never forgiven myself. The story somehow appeared in The Sun not long after, claiming I might miss the start of the season due to a 'golf buggy incident'. I don't know how it got out but it had.

Then the gaffer tells me the buggy needs paying for and I owed £1200, which I took on the chin and asked if they would just take it out of my wages. It remains, to this day, the most expensive round of golf I've played.

When we got back, Tony asked if I'd moved up yet from Barnsley and I said I had. But I knew he'd be checking in on me, so I asked a lad I knew from Macclesfield, who was now at Stoke, if I could use his address to tell the club that was where I'd moved to.

If I did that, I could claim my relocation money which was about £8,000. I got a few receipts together and handed them in and got paid shortly after. Meanwhile, we'd signed Richard Cresswell from Leeds and he was living near me in York so I started coming in with him to split the petrol.

Tony clocked us coming in for training one day and I think he probably suspected I hadn't moved. John Rudge was our sporting director at the time and he asked me if I'd moved in yet. I said yeah, I had and that it was good… a nice area and all that.

"How's the house?" he asked.

"Good as gold thanks John."

"That's funny," he said. "Every other house on your street is flooded."

"Fuckin' hell!" I said. "I'd better get off and check it."

Of course, they knew what the craic was, but nothing else was ever mentioned. They must have thought I was a cheeky fucker and just let me carry on.

I didn't play in our first game of the season away to Cardiff but started against Rochdale in the Carling Cup in midweek and lasted about an hour. We were live on *Sky* for our next game against Charlton and I was on the bench until the 74th minute with the score at 1-1. I'd only been on a few minutes when the ball came to me, I chopped it inside, megged the centre-half and buried it in the bottom corner for what turned out to be the winner.

I was thinking I might have half a chance of starting against Southampton the week after but I was back on the bench and again came on and scored a late goal in a 3-2 defeat.

So with my three-in-six loan spell the previous season and the two in two from the new season, I'd scored five goals in eight games, which is a decent return for any striker, especially as four goals had come off the bench. I thought that surely – surely – I'd be starting the next game, but I was back on the bench again! I'd always needed games to stay at peak fitness so starting sub every game meant I wasn't anywhere near my sharpest.

We were doing well so I could sort of understand why I wasn't getting a start and Sidibe was doing such a good job at being the second striker, there was no way Pulis could have dropped him. He worked his bollocks off and had the kind of mobility needed in that team, so although I would play my part, I was mainly coming off the bench during the 2007/08 season. That meant as the season went on, the less match-fit I was getting, but I liked Tony Pulis and I liked playing for Stoke so I got on with it, trained as best I could and tried my best when I got the chance.

The problem was, when Tony did throw me in, I was fucked after about an hour. I needed that four or five game run to hit top speed and that just wasn't happening.

Clare and I had got engaged the summer before and I knew that if we got promoted to the Premier League, I'd get a six-figure bonus and my wages would double. That would pay for our wedding – plus allow us to buy the new house she was after – so financially, it didn't make sense to rock the boat.

I also know Tony liked me being around the dressing room

and thought I was a good influence, which I enjoyed, too. We had a great set of lads. Steve Simonsen, Danny Higginbotham, Liam Lawrence, Richard Cresswell – plus that Rory Delap throw that I would have liked to have been on the end of on the odd occasion. We had a good set of honest, hard-working and experienced players who all got on and played well together. We didn't have many injuries, we were going well so if it ain't broke, don't fix it.

About midway through the season, we arranged a night out in London after our game against Crystal Palace. I told Clare I had a golf day planned for Wednesday and that's what the rest of the lads who were going out said as none of us wanted the hassle from the wives. There were maybe six of us plus Gab Zakuani's mate who came along – and turned out to be Dizzee Rascal, as I'd find out a few days later.

We won the game 3-1 and headed out to a nightclub. I remember we couldn't get into the Faces nightclub in east London, despite having music megastar Dizzee in our midst. I don't remember him getting many rounds in either!

Anyway, we eventually got back to our hotel at 5am, heading

straight for the bar. I had some breakfast about 7am and then stayed in the bar until 5pm that afternoon. We were all smashed but determined to carry on. After tea, Paul Dickov met up with us and we headed out again. Clare was ringing me intermittently, but I was three sheets to the wind when I was meant to be playing golf.

Finally, after about a 24-hour piss-up, we headed back to Stoke on the train where we had booked another hotel to stay at as we'd be training the next morning. Richard Cresswell was injured so when we got back, he asked if I fancied going out for a few. Some of the other lads headed home so I said: "Go on then!"

By 4am Thursday morning, we arrived back at the hotel with training to come – for me – in about seven hours. I'd still not spoken to Clare since my supposed golf day began and she'd been calling me constantly. So when I woke up after about five hours' sleep I had to take her next call.

"Where have you been?" she said.

I had to think on my feet. "I was arrested. I've been in a cell all night without my phone."

"Why didn't you let me know?" she asked. I said I was only allowed one call so had to inform the club where I was. It was inspired, and I think she bought the golf all day and arrest at night story – until she reads this!

I trained but was blowing out of my arse throughout the session and just wanted to get my head down for a few hours. I got showered and then drove back to Barnsley. Thursday night was always a date night out for me and Clare so as soon as I got back, she says: "We going out then?" All I wanted to do was sleep, but as I was still covering my tracks, I just tried to look enthusiastic and said yes. We went out and I just about made it through, though I was pushing food around my plate and counting the minutes down.

We were away to Bristol City on the Saturday so had another long journey to Stoke with no Richard Cresswell to take me in. Then we set off for Bristol where I came on for about 15 minutes having had probably six hours' sleep in four days. Not the best.

Towards the end of the season, I'd got a bit frustrated with Tony. I wasn't starting games and after a while, it starts to wear you down. I needed to be playing and thought I might be able to get out on loan for a few weeks just to get fit.

Then on the last day of the loan window, Tony told me two Championship clubs had come in to take me on loan. I said I was up for it and asked which clubs were interested. He said he'd let me know later. I got home and, knowing the window closed at 5pm, I waited for a call. And waited. And waited. Finally, the phone goes at 4.45pm. It was Tony, who said Plymouth wanted to take me on loan.

I said: "Plymouth? Fuckin' hell gaffer, it's miles away."

He said: "I know, but you can train with us on Mondays and Tuesdays, they'll fly you down on Wednesday, train with them Thursday and Friday – play Saturday – and then fly you back. It'll be for the last six weeks of the season."

I asked him how long I had to think about it and he said: "Fifteen minutes."

I hadn't spoken to Clare about this at all, but I said: "Yeah, fuck it – I'll do it."

He asked if I had a fax machine because I'd need one, but I didn't – so I had to find one quickly. I jumped in my car and headed for the only place I could think of – the library a couple of minutes away in the village. I burst through the door. Nobody else but the librarian was in there and I asked if I could borrow the fax machine and I'd explain why later.

It was 4.55pm and I still needed to receive the forms, sign them and fax them back. I tried, but it was 'Mission Impossible', and I probably missed the deadline by ten minutes in the end. That was as near as I got to becoming a Plymouth Argyle player, but having accepted the move, I was now raging that I'd not been told at the last minute.

Just 15 minutes earlier and I probably could have faxed the papers back in time, but the real reason was that – I think – Tony didn't really want me to go. It was a token gesture to keep me sweet but, as I say, he liked having me around the place. I went into training the next day still pissed off at what had happened, and my head was up my arse a bit.

At the end of the session, the fitness coach told me the gaffer had said I needed to do some extra running. I was still having a bit of a sulk and said: "Fucking what? Tell the gaffer to fuck off. I've got to catch a plane to Plymouth in 15 minutes."

I headed off home and thought I'd get the bollocking I probably deserved, but my punishment was a letter the next day telling me I'd been fined a week's wages and I wasn't in the squad for our next game. Not the first time that had happened. But I wasn't happy with getting a fine for that – it was too much, and I thought I had some justification given what had gone on the day before – so I took it to the PFA who got it reduced. It still cost me a bit, but it was less than it had been.

I think I was on the bench twice more after that and then I was out of the team altogether and playing reserve-team football. Even then, I managed to piss off the gaffer by continually turning up late. I got to one game against Wolves at 6.50pm for a 7pm kick-off. I was walking along the touchline with my washbag while the lads were just coming off the pitch from a pre-match warm-up. Then I got lost in Bradford and arrived with the game 35 minutes old. I was always getting myself into little scrapes like that. There was nothing malicious in it; it was just how I was.

By that time it was getting towards the end of the season and we were still right up there, even if I wasn't directly involved. It was proper squeaky bum time for me because I had so much riding on it with the wedding and a deposit for the new house, but as I was now out of the picture, I'd be playing no part.

I'd been the most used sub in the Championship with just four starts and 25 appearances from the bench, but with one game to go, we needed a point to go up automatically. The Britannia was rammed and while we needed just a point, Leicester needed to win to stay up. We scrapped and worked hard as we always had that season and ground out a 0-0 draw – but that was enough. It meant everything was sorted – the bonus, the wedding, the house, the lot.

I was now effectively a Premier League player, but I wondered how often I'd be used given I'd only started four in the Championship and had basically been frozen out for the last six weeks.

Still, now was time to celebrate and I went along to a hotel in Stoke where Richard Cresswell and some of his family were having a few beers. About five pints in, I thought, 'Fuck it, I'll ring Phil Brown'. He had taken Hull into the play-offs. I used a phone belonging to a mate of Cresswell's and called Brown and just started laughing when he answered it before hanging up. I know he tried that number for days after so mystery solved, Phil – it was me. As it turned out, Hull went up anyway which was brilliant for them. I was happy for the lads and the Hull fans who'd always been great with me.

We ended up going to Andy Wilkinson's nightclub until the early hours before about 10 of us headed out to Magaluf the following Tuesday. That was, as you can probably imagine, a lively break.

We were there for five days, but we headed home after four – we'd drunk the place dry and everyone had had just about enough. I remember returning to the hotel one evening to see Rory Delap swaying by reception, just mumbling.

The receptionist couldn't understand what he was saying but I caught the word 'key' so I asked her if he could have a key for his room and gave her his name. I asked her how long he'd been there, and she said: "About 40 minutes!"

It was far from the end for me, though – about three days after I returned to Barnsley it was time to head out with my mates for my stag do. We flew to Benidorm and blitzed it again. I wore a mankini for the first two days and didn't take it off once – slept in it, ate in it, drank in it... I dread to think what it must have smelled like. People were asking to have their picture taken with me. I'm stood there and more often than not with my cock and balls hanging out, too. Thank God social media wasn't everywhere back then! I had two tan lines up the side of my body where the mankini had been.

By day five I was in a bit of a pickle. We'd gone into a bar and I'd ordered a WKD Blue because it was the only thing I could think of that I might keep down. I had a sip, but I couldn't stomach it and decided to slope off to my room.

I felt like shit and lay down, but I couldn't sleep and started shivering and shaking. It was no wonder – I'd been on a bender for nine of the last 12 days and had been out day and night. I was in a right mess and was thinking about calling an ambulance, but because I didn't know how to, I didn't. It was probably just as well as they'd have almost certainly kept me in. That wouldn't have gone down too well at home.

I managed to get through the night and had a few sips of water in the morning as I started to come around again. It was a relief, but my own fault as I'd just been hammering it and my body was telling me it had had enough. I flew home, had a few quiet days and not long after I got married to Clare at an old priory in Wakefield.

It cost a fortune, but it was an incredible do and afterwards we headed out to New York, Las Vegas and Hawaii for three weeks on honeymoon. It had been a big summer – one of my biggest yet – and by the end of it, I went on the Atkins Diet for a week to try and shift a stone before it was time to start pre-season training again.

I doubted my future lay at Stoke, but I'd finally made it to the Premier League and had some serious thinking to do.

9

PREMIER LEAGUE – YOU'RE HAVIN' A LAUGH, PAL

> So I was lying on the bed with my arms out like Eddie The Eagle as the physio gave my triceps a rub. One of the lads sauntered in and was like, 'What the fuck is that?' He got the others to come in and have a look. I was settling in well

For any footballer carrying a bit of timber or not at the peak of their fitness, the worst thing you can have is the bleep test. Basically, run as far as you can for as long as you can, reaching targets timed by bleeps as the fitness coaches try and gauge where you're at. I dropped out before Level 9 and the keepers were still going by that point! You needed to get to a minimum of Level 14 and Russell Hoult and Steve Simonsen kept going as I reached my limit.

A goalkeeper's fitness and stamina level is usually a lot less than an outfield player, but the goalies were plodding on while I was gasping for oxygen, unable to take another step. I think the coaching staff could tell I'd enjoyed my summer.

We headed out to Austria again and I played a half here, a half there during the trip, but Dave Kitson had joined, and my chances of playing had receded even further. We started the Premier League season away to Bolton, but I wasn't in the squad, as expected, so had to watch from the stands.

I knew already I wouldn't be anywhere near the first-team and if I wasn't playing, I'd gradually get more unfit. And if I was used at any stage, I'd be a sack of shit. I needed to be playing.

We were well beaten by Bolton 3-1 on the opening day and then beat Aston Villa in our next game. I never thought Tony Pulis was going to turn around and say: "Enough's enough. Send for Parky!" at any stage, no matter how the season panned out. I'd be effectively tossing off a year of my career if I stayed at Stoke and even though I'd finally got to the top division, just being there wasn't enough.

The following Tuesday, we were away to Cheltenham in the League Cup and even though we knew there'd be changes, I was surprised to start the game and I scored in a 3-2 win. It would be the only time I ever played a game as a Premier League player because the next day, Tim called me to say Preston North End were interested in me. It was a relief because throughout my career, no matter how I'd been doing, I always feared that nobody would want me when I was available or my contract was running down.

Preston were offering a three year deal and Tim said their manager Alan Irvine wanted to meet me. I travelled to Preston and met with Alan and the Preston chairman Derek Shaw on the Thursday evening. We were having a meal at a restaurant and I hadn't eaten since noon. The meeting was at 8pm, so by that time, I was starving. I needed to see what they were ordering first before I decided. Dinner was on them and I was thinking, 'Should I fucking go for it here or what?', but Alan Irvine didn't order a starter and neither did the chairman, so it was mains only. Oh well…

We ate, chatted over this and that and things seemed to go well so they said they'd be in touch and I headed back to Stoke. I trained the following morning and was included in the squad away to Middlesbrough for the following day, knowing I'd be nowhere near the team or bench. Tim said I should take my car up to Middlesbrough just in case anything developed. There was only a day or so of the summer transfer window to go so I needed to be able to move quickly if I needed to. Preston did make an offer on the Friday, but Tim informed me Tony Pulis didn't want me to go! I couldn't work it out, so I went to see him to find out what his thinking was.

I said: "Gaffer, can I have a word?" He nodded.

"Why don't you want me to join Preston?"

He said: "Parky, look, I don't want you to go. I like having you around the place."

As frustrated as I was, I had to smile. "Gaffer, I'm 27. I'm not here to keep you entertained like some court jester."

He said he realised that, but argued that he enjoyed me being part of his squad. I told him that wasn't any good for me, even if I admit it was a decent thing to hear from your manager.

He said: "Well you're not getting any money to leave."

I told him I didn't want any money and that I'd be taking a £100,000-per-year pay cut to leave, so it was never about that. It was about playing football while I still had the opportunity. I just asked him to accept the bid, let me get off and we'd shake hands and leave on good terms.

Though it was the right thing to do for my career, I should have thought of the bigger picture because, in reality, from a financial point of view, it was a mistake.

He told me he'd speak to me later. We travelled to our hotel and at 7pm we had a team meeting ahead of the Middlesbrough game. As Tony went through his analysis, I got a text from Tim telling me to get to Preston because the deal was done. I wasn't sure what to do, so I stood up and raised my hand like a schoolkid and said: "Gaffer, I need to leave."

He said "okay" and I just said: "Right lads, all the best," went to my room to get my bag and then headed out for Preston. I arrived about 10pm, had a medical – more of a token gesture than a thorough medical because I hadn't passed a medical for about seven years – but I got through it and went to the hotel.

The chairman came with the contract which stated I'd be on a two-day loan which became permanent on the Monday because the FA offices were shut over the weekend. I was now a Preston player and was in the team for the match the next day. They paid about £350,000 for me with add-ons but, in hindsight, I probably should have gone there initially on a season-long loan. If I'd done that, my money would have stayed the same if Stoke had made the rest up and I'd have still had a Premier League contract. But I'd made my decision and now I just needed to get on with it.

I made my Preston debut against Charlton and even if I do say so myself, I was brilliant. I didn't score but I had a great game.

Around this time, me and Clare were trying for a baby and we were trying to time it exactly right, so I'd be off in the summer to help her when the baby was born. She had all these ovulation kits and dates planned out. She called me up at Coventry and told me the evening before the game.

I said I couldn't do anything about it just then, but after the game, we had to go to a wedding in Whitby – my ex-girlfriend Paula was getting married to one of my best pals from school – and we'd have to sort it then.

It was scorching hot at Coventry and I played the full 90 minutes, but I was crap. Alan Irvine had put me on a fitness regime because he told the coaches I needed to lose a bit of timber. So with the extra work, the heat and a full game, I was fucked. I was doing powerwalks every day on a treadmill and I was thinking, 'What am I doing here?'

It was boring as fuck, so the second time I took a paper with me to read and put it on the display in front of me. I think the physio probably realised then he had his work cut out for him. I'd done upper body weights on Thursday – something I'd never done before or ever wanted to do. By matchday, my triceps were killing me. I asked the physio to give my triceps a rub because I couldn't move my arms.

"Are you having a laugh? A rub on your triceps?" he said.

I said: "Yeah, you've killed me."

He said: "I've never done a rub on triceps in my life, pal."

I went: "I don't give a fuck. I need a rub on them."

So I was lying on my bed with my arms out like Eddie The Eagle as the physio gave my triceps a rub. One of the lads sauntered in and was like, 'What the fuck is that?' He got the others to come in and look and by now, I'm getting pelters as my arms are being massaged. I'd only been there a week but seemed to be settling in.

Anyway, I missed the wedding ceremony because of the game but drove to Whitby afterwards for the evening do. It took me about four hours to get there – Clare had gone up for the church bit with some friends – and I got there at about 9pm and went to our room at the hotel. Clare met me there and said: "Come on then."

I said: "Are you kidding me?" She said she was ovulating and I said: "I don't give a fuck if you're ovulating or not. I've just played 90 minutes, then driven four hours… we'll sort it later."

She said no, because I'd be pissed, and it wouldn't happen, so I had to get busy. We had friends waiting for us to take a taxi to the reception, so it was a proper SAS job – in and out as quick as possible – a two-minute wonder and job done. I wanted a drink by that time, too, but I was training the next day, so I couldn't go too mad. Of course, I ended up getting twatted. I woke up half-an-hour late the next morning and had to put my foot down, getting there just in time, but my arse was hanging out. As it happened, that was the night Clare fell pregnant, so it's just as well she did coerce me into it or everything might have been different.

There was a great group of lads at Preston and I'd felt at home straight away. Paul McKenna had been there years and he must have looked at me when I arrived and thought, 'Fuck me, what's that?' I could see as much in his face, but we ended up being good mates. We all got on well and once I'd found my feet, I suppose I became the bants ringleader.

So while everything was fine and dandy off the pitch, I couldn't score on it. I'm not sure what the Preston fans must have thought, but by early November, I still hadn't found the back of the net and I was dropped for a few games. It was the worst run of my career and though I was contributing in other ways, playing okay and working hard, I could fully understand Alan Irvine's thinking.

I was kicking my heels for about three weeks before I was recalled to the starting line-up against Barnsley, but the run went on and I didn't score in that game or against Cardiff City in the next. It didn't matter what I tried, nothing was working, and I'd now gone 15 games and three months without a goal.

Then, in early December, we were at home to Doncaster on a damp Tuesday evening at Deepdale. I was back on the bench and I just needed a break of some kind… anything because it was winding me up – but it was about to come to an end at long last. I came on after 76 minutes and six minutes later, I finally broke my duck and scored the only goal of the game. Thank fuck for that. It was a massive relief.

We were home to Birmingham City in our next game and I was back on the bench again, but I was okay because the pressure was off now. It was also our Christmas do day and I always had a bit of a spring in my step on Christmas do day, as you might imagine.

We were drawing 0-0 with 12 minutes to go and Irvine tells me to warm up because I'm going on. It was a tea time kick-off and live on Sky, so I went on and missed an easy chance within a few minutes. I wondered if I was about to go on another barren run, but on 90 minutes, Ross Wallace swung in a cross and Birmingham defender Liam Ridgewell missed it. The ball fell to me just behind and I cushioned it down with my chest and then tucked it away in the bottom corner.

Deepdale went mad, I'd scored back-to-back winners and

all was good in the world again. You always want to win on Christmas do day to get the evening off to a flyer and we were now in the mood to party, so headed to Liverpool as quick as we could for the weekend.

Alan Irvine put me back in the team and, though we lost 3-2 to QPR, I scored on Boxing Day against Derby County. I never drank on Christmas Day because if I did, I couldn't eat and that was one day I definitely wanted to eat. I'd scored three in four and felt I was starting to repay the gaffer's faith in me. I was far from prolific, but we were probably punching above our weight in the Championship.

At the start of January, Liverpool came to Deepdale in the FA Cup third round. They had a pretty strong team out, with the likes of Steven Gerrard, Javier Mascherano, Jamie Carragher and Xabi Alonso all on the pitch. They went 1-0 up early on when Albert Riera smashed one in.

We were chasing a goal in the second half when the ball went into their box. I challenged with Carragher and we both went down on the floor. We had a bit of a grapple on the ground as the ball came back into the box. Sean St Ledger headed it in, but the ref disallowed it for my tangle with Carragher. Fernando Torres came on as a sub and made it 2-0 in the last minute and we were out. Gutted.

After a collectively shit performance against Southampton in

February, Alan Irvine took us all away on a mid-season break to Benalmadena. He'd arranged a warm weather training camp and I'll never forget him saying: "And if you think it's a fucking holiday, you're wrong – it's not a fucking holiday!"

We had the Sunday and Monday off and then flew out on the Tuesday and trained that same afternoon. We rested for a few hours, then had our dinner in the evening and when we'd finished, I asked the lads if anyone wanted to walk down to the marina for a coffee.

About 10 of us ended up going and we headed out with the best of intentions as we entered a bar near the marina. The waiter came over and asked what everyone wanted, so it was "Coffee, Coke…" then he came to me and I said: "Fuck it, I'll have a pint." As I was only the third to be asked, it had a knock-on effect and seven of the lads ended up having a pint.

The waiter came back 20 minutes later. "Same again?" I said yes. After that, the lads that had been on coffees and Coke said they were getting off, while the rest of us carried on. By about half eight, we'd had about five pints each and – bearing in mind it wasn't a holiday – we weren't doing too bad.

I could see a guy outside the bar selling souvenirs, hats and necklaces so I nipped out and bought some glasses, a hat, a Hawaiian shirt, necklaces and a few puppets and quickly got dressed before going back into the bar. I shouted over to the lads: "Remember, it's not a fucking holiday, this!" They started pissing themselves and I added: "Just let me do the jokes, Al!"

We had another couple and then headed back to the hotel. We weren't in too bad shape, and we were back in our rooms by 11pm. Next day, we trained at 8am, had lunch and then trained again at 4pm. We showered, went back to our rooms for a rest and came back down for dinner, just as we'd done the previous night. I asked if anyone fancied going for a coffee at the marina again and the same seven lads all headed out again. We probably had about eight pints each this time – again, not bad seeing as this wasn't a holiday!

Next day, we were a bit more fuzzy-headed than the first time but, in Groundhog Day fashion, we went through the same routine and after dinner, I said to the lads who we'd by now named MM7 – fuck knows why – "Are we out or what?'" And off again we headed to the marina. This time we found ourselves a little back street bar – it was February so there was hardly anyone in. We were sat around a big table and we threw a few £20 notes in the middle and kept the beers flowing. It was the best holiday I'd been on in ages.

After a while, one of the lads looks at his watch and says: "Fuck! It's 3.30am!" We'd been in the bar for seven hours and had training in five hours, so we had one more for the road and headed back to the hotel.

We went outside and there was just one taxi across the street, so everyone bolted to it but he would only take four. Chris Brown had jumped in the boot, but the driver got out and told him to get out and that he'd ring another cab for the rest of us.

Of course, our driver gets lost on the way back to the hotel and we didn't get back to our rooms until 5am with breakfast to come at half past seven.

I was rooming with Chris Sedgwick whose alarm went off a couple of hours later. He looked over at me and just started pissing himself. I asked him what was up, and it turned out I'd gone to bed fully clothed but somehow, I'd also acquired the taxi driver's jacket.

Chris asked what the fuck I was wearing, but I was just hoping the driver's takings weren't in this jacket or else I'd been in a spot of bother. Thank God, the pockets were empty. Those of us who'd been out were not in a good state at breakfast and six of us ended up in the same passing drill.

Billy Jones was injured but the rest of MM7 stumbled through training that had resembled an Under-7s session. We must have been stinking of beer, but we got through it and were keen to get back to the room ahead of the afternoon session and get our heads down.

But then Alan Irvine called us together and said: "Right lads, you've worked well this week. We'll have lunch at 12 and you can have the afternoon around the pool and have a drink."

My heart sank. I wasn't in the mood for any more drink and so I headed back to the room to get my head down. I went down later, and the lads were all enjoying themselves and this time, we were fine to go out and have a beer in the evening – and I suppose it goes without saying that we did.

The break did us good and I scored in each of our next four games as we started to build some momentum. Towards the end of the season, we had a shout at getting in the play-offs and were home to Cardiff, who were above us in the table with three games left to play. I'd spoken to Jay Bothroyd before the game – I knew him from a month's loan at Stoke but he was now at Cardiff. He was a complete ball-bag by the way – a self-opinionated prick who is right up there with Phil Brown for me. I said Cardiff had a real chance of going up because they were second or third and had a game or two in hand. Bothroyd, modest as ever, said: "Yeah, we'll do your lot today, then we'll win Tuesday and we'll be sound."

We ended up beating them 6-0.

We had a meeting after the game and as I came out of the changing rooms, one of the lads said Cardiff manager Dave Jones was going ballistic in the away dressing room. I had a little listen at the door just in time to hear him say: "You're a fucking disgrace. You let those two fat cunts up front score and bully you. They wiped the floor with you!"

You didn't need to be a rocket scientist to work out he was on about me and Neil Mellor, so I had a little chuckle to myself and as I moved away, Jones stormed out. His chairman Peter Ridsdale was waiting for him, so I just moved out of the way.

Ridsdale asked Jones to go in our physio room for a quick chat and I thought, 'Fuck this,' I took my top off, opened the physio room door and Jones and Ridsdale glared over at me. I said: "Oh, I'm very sorry – very sorry – I'm just looking for my diet sheet and the physio said I'd left it in here." Peter Ridsdale had a little smirk on his face and though Dave Jones was raging, I could tell he wanted to laugh.

The last game of the season, we were home to QPR and Sheffield Wednesday were playing Cardiff. If we won and Cardiff didn't, we'd get into the play-offs and they wouldn't. It was a bit tense and still 0-0 in both games with about 35 minutes played, then the QPR centre-half plays it back, but it was short. I managed to nip in, go around the keeper and though Neil Mellor was free in the middle and it was a ridiculous angle, I decided to go for it. It skimmed one post and went in off the other to put us 1-0 up. Happy days.

Patrick Agyemang made it 1-1 after half-time, but in the other game, Sheffield Wednesday were beating Cardiff 1-0.

We knew if we scored another goal, we'd have a great chance of ending in sixth. There was 15 minutes to go, nothing was happening, and we didn't look like scoring so when the ball went out of play on the left near the QPR box, I thought, 'Fuck it, I'll launch it in'.

I'd never taken a long throw in my life, but I waved all the lads forward, kicked the advertising board out of the way to give myself a better run up and then slung it into the box. It went miles – Rory Delap-style. The keeper went up for it, spilled it and Sean St Ledger bundled the ball into the net for the winner. A few moments later it was confirmed Cardiff had lost and the fans ran onto the pitch because we'd made the play-offs.

We had the same goal difference as Cardiff, but we'd ended up scoring one more goal than them and that was all we needed. That 12-goal swing on the goal difference from when we beat them 6-0 had done it.

Three games away from the Premier League, we had Sheffield United in the play-offs and because of the way we'd snuck in on the last day, we thought we might have a bit of a chance. There always seems to be a dark horse who sneaks up on the rails so maybe this time it would be us.

We had the first leg at home on the Friday night and played really well, went one up through Sean St Ledger and then I hit the post. We deserved to win, but Brian Howard scored for the Blades just after the restart and it ended 1-1.

There was still everything to play for at their place and we still fancied it, but Greg Halford scored an outrageous header from the edge of the box on the hour and though we almost scored right at the death, that was the end of that dream – we lost 2-1 on aggregate and missed out. The play-offs are incredible if you go up but sickening if you don't.

So, back to the drawing board...

10

ALL CHANGE AT PRESTON

> By halfway, I trailed so far back that it was embarrassing. I was trying my balls off, but it was no use. Alan Irvine dropped back and acted as my pacemaker. I was thinking, 'This guy is 50 and he's my pacemaker? Fuck me, I've hit rock bottom'

We'd timed everything perfectly and the baby was due on June 7, 2009 – the date of our first wedding anniversary. Clare was trying all sorts to bring on the birth – acupuncture, curries, the lot – but with no joy. Because of pre-season starting in July and trying to get the most out of me being home, we went to hospital to see if there was any way they could start her off, but they basically said, 'no chance'. They said the only thing they could do was a sweep, so a few days later we went back in and they gave her a sweep before we went home to see if anything happened.

I dropped Clare back home because I was golfing in the evening and there was no point in just hanging around, doing nothing and probably annoying her. I had my phone with me and if anything happened, I could be back in 20 minutes.

I was on the fourth hole when she called to tell me she felt like something was happening. I said: "Oh. Right. Well, I'm golfing. Do you want me to come back?" She said no, and I just said to call back if she did. Three holes later, she calls me again and says the feelings had increased.

I was playing quite well and was halfway through my round so I said: "Look, give it an hour and call me again, love." I think I was on the 15th hole and my phone goes for a third time. She said I needed to get back, so this time I made my apologies and got home for about half-eight.

Clare had rung the hospital, but they said not to bother going in as she'd be nowhere near ready. By midnight, we decided enough was enough and headed in. We sat there for three hours with nobody really doing very much. I might be aggressive on the pitch, but I'm quite placid off it. However, I was starting to rage a bit at the time we'd been waiting – even though now I know it wasn't that long at all. The only time I'd spent in hospitals was when I needed a knee op and those had been private and in and out jobs. This was my first proper experience of the NHS and I was ranting about all the taxes I'd paid and this, that and the other. Finally, a doctor turns up, measures her and she was just one centimetre dilated!

He wasn't best pleased at being summoned up and told us we'd be better off going home as there was nothing doing and wouldn't be for a while. So we headed home, managed to get a bit of sleep and by noon the next day, Clare was starting to struggle with the pain, so we went back to hospital.

She got measured and she was now just two centimetres dilated! I was thinking, 'Fuck me, she's taking the piss here!' They said we could either go home or go and wait in the birthing room, so I said to Clare: "Fuck it. Let's get in the birthing room. I'm not traipsing here and there all day." Clearly it was me that was suffering here!

We went in but although the pain was getting worse, she wasn't dilating any further. By midnight, she was just four centimetres dilated and I started to wonder if this baby was ever going to come.

Five hours later, she was finally in a position to start pushing. The nurse asked me if I wanted to have a look below as things progressed, so I did, and I asked her: "What's that?" She said: "That's was the baby's head." I thought that there was no way on earth that baby was coming out – how could it? It looked impossible.

Clare was pushing and becoming exhausted and the doctor was starting to get concerned, but he told her to try one more big push. About ten minutes later, at 7.10am on June 10, 2009, my son, Oliver Parkin, entered the world. He was about 8lbs 10 ounces – a big lad like his dad – but he was a little cracker.

I'd read up on births and what is best to do so I whipped off my shirt and put him on my chest straight away. Clare was absolutely knackered. She'd been in labour for about 30 hours and needed to rest, but the little man was finally here, safe and well and I was now big daddy. I had three or four weeks at home helping Clare before pre-season kicked in and it all started again.

Having joined Preston a few weeks after the season had started, the 2009/10 campaign would be my first pre-season under Alan Irvine and I wasn't sure what to expect. We were all a bit nervous about what was to come.

As ever, the lads were asking each other what they'd been doing over the summer. Some had been in the gym regularly, some had been running, others had been careful with their diet, but when anyone asked me, the answer was always the same – "Absolutely fuck all."

As usual, there would be some who thought I was joking and others who probably thought I was mad, but it was the truth. It had become something of a tradition.

We found out on the first day that the gaffer wanted to take us down to Lytham St Annes to train on the beach. I wasn't happy. Kids and donkeys like beaches, not footballers. It turns out we were to do a long distance run and that, to me, is like Kryptonite to Superman. I loathed distance running with a passion. I can do sprints all day long, but running for more than that killed me.

We were told we had to run to the pier which was 2.2 miles away and then split between running and walking coming back. We set off and, as I always did, I started as fast as I could and then just tried to hold on for dear life. For the first minute I was up there with the leaders, then my thighs started to explode and I gradually fell further and further back.

By halfway, I tailed so far back that it was embarrassing. I was trying my balls off, but it was no use. Alan Irvine dropped back (he probably caught a bus) and acted as my pacemaker. I was thinking, 'This guy is 50 and he's my pacemaker? Fuck me, I've hit rock bottom.'

We had 14 minutes to do the first run and then rest for four minutes before we headed back. Irvine was talking to me as we ran, trying to gee me up and forget the pain, but I could barely breathe and had spit flying out everywhere whenever I opened my mouth. We arrived after 17 and a half minutes and I was close to death. I tried to catch my breath, but then the assistant manager says we all had 30 seconds before we went again. My ears pricked up and between gasps I said: "What do you mean 30 seconds?"

He said that was when we would set off back. I asked if he was kidding but sure enough they soon started heading back up the beach. I plodded back and even threw in a few sprints, which I was fine with, but as first days go, it was a shitter.

All that pre-season was hard under Big Al, but he knew I was trying and that was good enough for him. So long as I kept doing my best, there would never be a problem from his perspective. We went to Austria for pre-season where a small piece of history was made as I turned a night out down. We'd been working so hard that after a couple of days, Alan Irvine said that we could go out at night and have the third day off.

But the training had been intense, I was still travelling two hours to Preston and two hours back every day, plus I'd had so many sleepless nights with the baby that a night in bed resting was, for the first time in my life, quite appealing. I saw Alan at breakfast and, for once, I looked the freshest and most rested

– the model pro, if you will. He said: "You missed a good night, Parky," and I said: "Gaffer, I've come here to get fit, not get pissed." He just laughed. I wonder why.

The 2009/10 season began, and we were doing okay, but were hovering around mid-table. I'd scored about five goals in 11 games by mid-October but – and I've no idea what it was about autumn – I then went on a 10-game run without scoring. We didn't have a particularly good festive period and after a 3-0 defeat to Nottingham Forest and then a 1-0 loss to Sheffield United, I got a text from one of the lads saying Alan had been sacked.

I was gutted in all honesty because I knew he liked me and he was a good, honest guy. He knew what I could do and, more importantly, what I couldn't do, so I was devastated to see him go. The Preston fans weren't happy, either.

I was scared shitless of him in a way that when he gave you a particular stare, the blood froze in your veins. I remember once making up a story that I'd been in a car crash just to avoid one of his bollockings.

I always left it to the last possible minute to leave home for training so if I hit any traffic along the way, I was fucked. On the day in question, I'd had a late night with Oliver and when I woke up, it had been snowing heavily. I had a rear-drive BMW and it was useless in the snow, so I decided the best way was to avoid the M62 and go through Huddersfield instead. It was even worse.

It got to the point where I knew there was no chance I'd make training and had to think on my feet, so I called the assistant manager and said I'd been involved in a car crash.

He asked if I was okay, said not to worry and I thought that was the end of that. The lads, however, weren't having it and wanted to fine me £250 for missing training.

I refused and pleaded my innocence, telling Callum Davidson, the fines manager, I wasn't paying. He asked why not. I said: "Fuck me. A car slid into me. What am I supposed to do?"

It was total fabrication, but the more I said it out loud, the more I actually believed it! He said they'd put it to a vote at the pre-match meal on Friday and I agreed. We finished dinner and I had to put my case across to the lads. I had a flipchart, markers, the lot. I drew roads and explained how I'd been hit by another car and that there had been nothing I could do.

I went into great detail as I presented my defence, and while some of the jury could tell it was utter bullshit, others weren't sure, and the vote was neck and neck. I think Sean St Ledger was wavering. I pleaded with him to do the right thing and he just said: "Yep, 100 per cent true." Case closed.

So Big Al was gone, and Rob Kelly took over as caretaker.

While I always stayed up in Preston the night before a home game, it was New Year weekend and I decided I'd drive in for our FA Cup tie against Colchester on the morning of the game. Clare's family were up from Weymouth so we had a few drinks. I slept in, got up at 11, looked out of the window and, once again, thick snow had fallen in the night. I got dressed and set off as quickly as I could, but the M62 was chaos.

By half 12, I knew I was going to be really late, so I called Rob Kelly and told him what had happened and where I was. Had it been Big Al, he'd have wiped the floor with me, but Rob just asked me to keep him posted. I was sliding all over the place and driving like a mad man, but I told Rob I would be there in time. Sure enough, I walked in at 1.55pm, five minutes before the team sheets were exchanged.

He said he would put me in the starting XI and I ended up scoring a hat-trick. Rob's faith had saved me and I couldn't have started much better under him. My goal drought had ended and two games later Darren Ferguson took over as our new manager. It was clear by that stage we wouldn't be troubling the promotion places that season, so his first job was to trim the wage bill down by deciding which players he wanted and those he didn't as he looked ahead to next season.

The ones he wanted to get rid of, he completely fucked off and had to train with the youth team. Neil Collins, Neil Mellor, Richard Chaplow and Chris Sedgwick were among those sent to train with the kids – they were experienced Championship players, but Fergie was trying to piss them off so they'd leave.

It was harsh but it happens in football and each manager has their own way of doing things. If he could trim £30,000 off the wage bill, he'd probably been told he'd be given some of it back – maybe £20,000 per week in wages – to bring in his own players. Gradually, the lads who were frozen out started moving on, but I'm not sure whether Ferguson was ever given any money to strengthen the team. If that was the case, in my eyes he was sort of stitched up.

I ended up with 12 goals from 43 appearances that season, which was an okay return. I'd had two years at Deepdale and had another to come and the new manager seemed happy enough to have me. Beyond that, I wasn't sure what was on the horizon.

11

POLES
APART

> *I folded all my clothes neatly as you did when you were at the swimming baths as a kid, then put them under my arm and calmly walked out to where the pole was, placed my clothes on the floor and then ushered the lasses away*

My marriage started to break down. I was gambling more heavily than ever, and Clare knew something was going on and hadn't been happy with me for a while.

I'd had the wrong mentality for too long and I think she'd just had her fill of it. When Oliver was born I didn't think I needed to change my life in any way. Clare could stay at home with the baby and while she couldn't go out I still thought, as the breadwinner, I should be able to. It was the way the old boys in the working men's clubs in Barnsley would think, but I should have known better. That's where my head was at back then and it got to a point where I was gambling pretty much every day.

At some stage, Clare must have found one of my bank statements. There was a withdrawal of £15,000 that I'd owed to a bookie who placed all my bets remotely, with me settling at the end of the month. I'd been chasing losses, lost even more and I'd had to withdraw the money and carry it around Barnsley in a bag for the guy I owed it to.

When she challenged me, I told her the truth and she went ballistic. She insisted it stopped now or else there'd be consequences. I agreed I would, but I didn't. Clare was on high alert now, and she found another statement a few weeks later with another £5,000 withdrawal and told me that if I didn't stop, she was off with the baby.

She was right. It had got completely out of hand but I was weak. As an example, during the previous season we'd been at home to Scunthorpe United and I'd backed Roger Federer to win the US Open the night before. He'd won five US Opens in a row – every match for five major tournaments – and he was 4/9 so I stuck £4,500 on him to win – the biggest bet I'd ever had. I had a game the next day and there I was, still up at four in the morning watching this final – and he gets beat by Juan Martin del Potro! I was like, 'How's your fucking luck?' My first bet on tennis and Federer goes down three sets to two. As with all gamblers, you're then chasing your losses and making it worse. So I was on something of a final warning with Clare and rightly so.

Back at Preston, I felt I'd done alright for Darren Ferguson. He seemed to like me as a player and as a person so I was happy to stay put for at least another year – but that was until Barnsley started showing an interest in me. Manager Mark Robins and his assistant had been to have a chat and see if I might be up for a move back to Oakwell. He said he wanted me to join them if they could agree a fee. They were willing to pay £300,000 and I really fancied going back home and not having the four-hour round trip commute every day.

But this was where my marital problems crossed over with my career. Clare and I were arguing more and more and by May we were really struggling. After one massive row I just said: "Right, I'm off!" I packed a bag and headed to a hotel in the next village where I'd grown up.

I went into a working men's club in Ardsley and stayed in there pretty much all day. I was wrecked and at some stage, I lost my shirt. I staggered the 800 yards to my hotel wearing just my shorts and flipflops and as I went in, there were two foreign guys stood outside smoking. I didn't pay them any attention and staggered inside to get changed and head into town. Two minutes later I was in a taxi heading out.

The next day, I was driving to Preston when I got a call from my agent. He said: "What the fuck were you doing yesterday?"

I asked him what he meant.

He said: "I've had a phone call from Mark Robins saying you went into a hotel last night, blind drunk with no shirt on."

It turned out the two guys outside the hotel were a couple of agents of Barnsley players and they'd recognised me in a right state and told Mark Robins the next day. I explained to Tim that I'd had a massive row and left Clare then just lost my head and gone out drinking, He told me he'd relay that to Mark Robins and that everything would be okay.

A few days later, I went back home and we tried to patch things up, but that was the beginning of the end, even if it would take a while longer before we split up for good.

A few days after our final game of 2009/10, I had an arthroscopy on my knee. It was just a trim to get rid of any floating cartilage. I had the operation on the Wednesday and it would take three or four weeks to mend.

It was all happening. My mate Craig was having his stag do

in Krakow three days after my op and I wasn't planning on missing the trip. I went in on Friday to let the physio check the wound. He knew what I was planning as I'd mentioned it a few days earlier and he said: "Parky, on no account can you go on that stag do. You've just had an operation so you'll need to come back in on Monday."

I said that was no bother and left. The stag party would last from early Saturday morning until Tuesday, so the timing couldn't have been any worse for me. I went home and I told Clare the physio had told me I couldn't go. She said that she agreed.

Then I added: "But I'm going to go anyway."

She asked how so I told her I'd leave in the morning and fly back Sunday night so nobody would be any the wiser. I booked my flight for Sunday and left the next morning for Krakow. We started drinking first thing and were out all day.

I was hobbling around a bit and we got back at daft o'clock in the morning. I was rough as a badger's arse when I woke up on the Sunday but I figured the only thing that would make me feel better was to carry on drinking. I wasn't flying back until 8pm and I reasoned that if I didn't drink, I'd just feel shit all day whereas if I just kept going, I'd be right by the time I flew home. Parky logic.

By 2pm and after four hours of beer, I'd started to get back into it and was feeling on top form. By 4pm I was counting the hours down because I'd have to leave for the airport soon, but I was back in the swing and in no mood to call it a day.

I rang Clare and told her I was staying another night and that I'd be flying home first thing on Monday morning. Then I turned my phone off and had told Clare if she needed me, to phone one of the lads. Before I did, I texted Jacko, the Preston physio, saying that I wouldn't be going in on Monday. I added: "Everything will become clear soon," making out I was talking to another club.

I went out Sunday night to a bar that was in a sort of cellar. It had a pole dancing area in the corner and by this point, we were well on our way. There were three lasses dancing around the pole and I had a brainwave, so headed to the toilets, didn't say anything to the lads, and once in the cubicle, stripped off.

I folded all my clothes neatly as you did when you were at the swimming baths as a kid, then put them under my arm and calmly walked out to where the pole was, placed my clothes on the floor and then ushered the lasses away. Then I started to pole dance, swinging myself around the pole naked. I could see the lads and they must have been thinking, 'What the fuck?' I'd only had an operation a few days before, but I was enjoying myself too much.

The next day I remembered what I'd done and just shook

my head. What was I doing? Thank God there was no social media as they'd have had a field day with me if anyone had taken any pictures that night. I turned my phone back on and saw a message from Clare saying: "Call me, you're in bother." I rang her to see what was wrong and she said she'd tried to call me earlier, but there was a message saying, 'This phone is unavailable.'

I said that was no problem, but then she said: "Yeah, but the message was in Polish."

There was another text from Baz, the other physio at Preston, just saying: "Where are you?" It turned out Jacko was away and hadn't got the message I sent, and it was Baz who was in on the Monday morning – he'd come in, I wasn't there, and he didn't know why.

The next message was from Darren Ferguson saying: "Parky, ring me ASAP." Now I had a problem. I'd done it again – nothing too outrageous but I'd landed myself in the shit yet again. I was thinking I'd probably lose a week's wages and this, that and the other, so I got my stuff together, jumped in a taxi for the airport and called Fergie.

"Hi gaffer, you alright?"

"I bet I'm a lot better than you," he said. "Good weekend in Krakow?"

I told him I knew I shouldn't have gone but he just said he

needed to speak to me. I told him I was on my way home and that I'd call in the next morning to see him.

The next day, I went in and he said: "Look, we've had this bid for you but I don't want you to leave."

Barnsley had offered £300,000 but Preston wanted £500,000 and, in the end, they were miles apart and that was the end of my hopes of going home. I'd set my heart on going back to Barnsley but the deal was off and I needed to get my head straight again. I had to try and save my marriage before anything else but things were too far gone by that stage and though I didn't know it, I was heading towards a dark place that I'd never been to before.

That summer Clare and I finally separated and I moved out of our house, leaving her and Oliver to live there. I moved in with Chris Brown from Preston and my routine would be to go to training, drive back to Barnsley and have Oliver until it was his time for bed and then drive back to Manchester where Chris lived. I'd do that four or five times a week, but at least the split hadn't been acrimonious in any way.

Clare and I still got on but we were better apart. I concluded it had taken me longer than it should have done to get used to becoming a dad. I'd felt I should still be able to do what I wanted to do, which I realise was wrong, but it was how it was at the time. If nothing else, Clare and I remained friends, it wasn't bitter and I got to see my son for four or five hours, four days (two of which were sleepovers at my house) a week.

Back at Preston, I'd got over the Barnsley move collapsing, had got up to speed in pre-season and started what would be my third and probably final season at Deepdale. Fergie was still in charge, but the 2010/11 campaign couldn't have started much worse.

We lost our first six Championship games and were rock bottom. Looking back at the teams we played – Swansea, Burnley, Sheffield United and Wigan to name but four – we'd played some decent sides. We also lost to Nottingham Forest and Norwich City so the pressure was really on the gaffer and all the lads.

But as shit as it looked, we probably should have had as many as 10 points out of the first 18 – maybe more. Okay, we were dicked 4-1 at Swansea on the opening day but we conceded a goal on 74 minutes to lose 1-0 at Sheffield United; we were 3-1 up at Burnley with six minutes to go but ended up losing 4-3; we were ahead against Nottingham Forest at half-time but lost 2-1 with another late goal costing us and after being

1-0 up at Wigan, conceded two in the last three minutes to lose 2-1. It was unreal how many points we'd tossed away. I was joint top scorer with Keith Treacy and, in fairness, Darren Ferguson never panicked. I think he knew we weren't far off and against Coventry, the tide began to turn.

We won 2-1 at the Ricoh Arena – our first victory of the season – and then were away to Leeds United – our sixth away game out of the first eight matches (and another reason we hadn't started that well).

We travelled to Elland Road and in no time at all, we were 4-1 down. I'd put us ahead after five minutes but with 39 played, I was thinking I would be chasing around for an hour for fuck all. But even though this sounds a bit corny, there was something in the air that night and when I scored again just before the break, I think we all felt that – for some reason – we could turn it around.

Ten minutes into the second half, Keith Treacy scores our third direct from a corner and four minutes after that, we were awarded a penalty. I'm on a hat-trick so I tell Callum Davidson to give me the ball, but he said he was the penalty taker and, in fairness, he scored to make it 4-4.

I got my third a couple of minutes after and ran to the corner where our fans were going mad, and then Iain Hume made it 6-4 not long after. It was the most surreal game of my career and I think it's one the Preston fans remember me best for. I scored seven in our first 12 games and even though we'd made a shit start, I was doing my job and scoring goals. I never took my home life into games and what happened away from football stayed away. I was lucky that I could switch off like that. But we never really recovered from that bad start and I went on a run of no goals in eight during my favourite season of autumn, when every day was like Halloween for me.

It was a frustrating spell, but in one game at home to Cardiff, I let things get the better of me. The Cardiff fans had been giving me shit and I had built up a lot of frustration over the past few months so when Michael Tonge put us 1-0 up, I grabbed the ball out of the net and leathered it into their fans. I still don't know why I did it.

I didn't think any more about it until I got into work on the Monday and one of the coaches came up and said I had to attend a meeting on Thursday, so I said: "Oh, okay – who with?" He said it was the club solicitor. Apparently when I'd kicked the ball into the Cardiff fans, I'd broken some guy's arm. I said: "No way! Seriously? I must have caught it well!"

I met the solicitor, told him I'd meant to lash the ball back into the net – even though it was blatantly obvious I hadn't meant to do that at all – and he took a statement from me. That was the last I heard of it. Or so I thought.

Meanwhile, Clare and I were considering getting back together again around Christmas, if not for ourselves, at least for Oliver. I had six months left on my contract and I was starting to think about life away from Preston. Tim called me to say a couple of clubs were interested in me and they turned out to be Sheffield Wednesday and Cardiff City. Wednesday were in League One and now managed by Alan Irvine. They were going well and, geographically, it would have been perfect. But Cardiff were second in the Championship and paying £100,000 a year more in wages so, financially, that made more sense.

I didn't want to leave Oliver behind so I said to Clare that I'd only go to Cardiff if she came with me. It was probably too early to make a commitment like that but football sometimes forces your hand and when she said she would come, I agreed to sign for Cardiff. It was the chance of a new start somewhere else and everything seemed right – but it would turn out to be one of the worst decisions of my life…

12

SNAKES AND LADDERS

I scored an incredible volley on my debut... although Bellamy wasn't playing with Tevez any more, I think even Carlos would have been happy with that goal and dare I say, Bellers might have thought that I wasn't as bad as he'd first imagined. I suppose you'd have to ask him!

I travelled to Cardiff for a medical and reasoned I could probably be back in Barnsley for a dinner/dance with Clare by the evening. I thought that if I left South Wales at 3pm latest, I'd still be home for 8pm with plenty of time to go out. Not for the first time, things didn't go to plan.

I failed the medical because of my knee. I wondered if the move might collapse but Dave Jones said he still wanted me to sign for him – partly because he was fed up of me scoring against Cardiff!

The owner Vincent Tan was in Malaysia so I had to wait around to see if it would happen or not, but Dave Jones was adamant it would and around 8pm, I finally became a Cardiff City player and signed the contract.

Clare had travelled back earlier and went to the dinner on her own. I got back at about 11pm and she returned with food from the do. I sat eating my New Year's Eve meal in the front room watching TV. Rock 'n' roll!

I didn't play for the first two weeks because of my knee injury but eventually I met the Cardiff lads and went out for my first training session with them. I was next to Craig Bellamy in the changing room and he must have looked at me and wondered where the club was heading.

He was on loan from Manchester City who weren't without a bob or two and signing top players from all around the world, but now he was back at his hometown club and in walks Jon Parkin. I doubt he even knew who I was. He had to have been thinking along the lines of, 'We're trying to get promoted and we've just signed that?'

On that first day's training, I was in Bellers' team in some shape drill we were doing. Somebody played the ball into him and he played it around the corner to me. I held the defender off and played it to the midfielder and as I do, Bellers starts shouting at me, telling me I should have given him the ball back. I thought I'd done my job there, so I shouted back: "Whoa, whoa! Wait a minute, pal. You're not playing with Carlos Tevez, now. He cost £35million and I cost a hundred grand so you need to bear that in mind when you're playing with me."

From that moment on, me and Bellers got on just fine. I think he liked people sticking up for themselves and we never had a problem after that.

Cardiff were in a good position and I knew that if they went up, my money would double. In all honesty that's the only reason I signed and while Cardiff fans may not thank me for that, it's the truth. First, we had to get promoted but I knew if we did, I could go on loan to a club in the north of England for the season because I was under no illusions that I was good enough to play in the Premier League.

Cardiff put me up in a hotel to begin with and things started well when I scored an incredible volley away to Norwich after just seven minutes of my debut. We were second and they were third and though Bellers wasn't playing with Tevez any more, I think even Carlos would have been happy with that goal. And dare I say it, Bellers might have thought that I wasn't as bad as he'd first imagined. I suppose you'd have to ask him!

We flew back to Cardiff and the captain Mark Hudson said the lads were going for a night out when we got back and asked if I was up for it. Fucking right I was. I got absolutely trollied and remember being sick in the taxi, but as the training session the following day was at the hotel I was staying at, I only had to roll out of bed, jog around a bit and that was that. My sort of session.

There were some good lads at the club. One of them, Michael Chopra, had gambling problems that were a couple of notches up on me and his addiction is widely known in football. The thing with Chops is that, he's a nice kid, but he's like a 14-year-old trapped in a man's body. The things that he did weren't the sort of things he should have been doing as a promising young footballer – like playing PlayStation until 4am in the morning the day before a game. He thought that was alright, but as a lad, as I say, he was a nice kid.

I didn't really get involved in the card school but before one game there must have been about £800 in the middle and Jlloyd Samuel (who is sadly no longer with us), Paul Quinn and Chops were in the hand. Jlloyd got to a point where he just said: "That's me done" and came out of it but Chops must have already owed Quinny two grand from previous games.

In the end it was just those two playing for the pot. Quinny looked as if he was about to fold then said: "Okay, I'll see you."

Chops must have thought he was bluffing and said: "I tell you what – I'll spin you for that two grand I owe you."

So Chops would either clear his debt completely, or end up losing about £4,000 in total. It turned out Quinny had three of a kind and Chops had a run, so Quinny won. And that was just on the way to a game! Of course, I was no saint when it came to gambling but Chops was letting it ruin his career.

As for Bellers, he was someone who people get the wrong idea about. His one failing, if you could call it that, was just that he wanted to win that much he thought everyone else should have the same mentality. It could come across as rude and arrogant but that was my impression of him and I respected the way he was – it was just his delivery he needed to work on!

The club had found a family house for Clare, Oliver and me a few weeks after I'd signed and after sorting a nursery out, they moved in. We were at least going to give it a go for his sake. As far as my place in the pecking order at Cardiff was concerned, I soon realised I'd been signed as a squad player more than anything else. After my scoring debut at Norwich, I played against Stoke in the FA Cup, losing 2-0 at home, and after that, Jay Bothroyd returned to fitness. It seemed clear I'd been signed as his back-up and I don't think I started another game that season. I was coming off the bench here and there, but I went 12 games without a goal because I couldn't get the run of games I needed to really get into my stride.

Dave Jones had brought in a few young lads throughout the season and some came on loan such as Jlloyd Samuel, Danny Drinkwater, Stephen Bywater, Jay Emmanuel-Thomas and Aaron Ramsey, so he could certainly spot a player. But there were some who came in who were just there for a piss-up and didn't do much for the team – not all of them, but some. Some of them were just kids and they weren't that arsed about Cardiff going up and it sort of killed us a bit.

We'd tailed off badly in the league and we ended up missing out on automatic promotion by just four points after winning only seven of our last 16 games.

But the season was far from over. We had still made the play-offs and went to Reading in the first leg and got a 0-0 draw. So we were all set to finish the job off at the Cardiff City Stadium and with more than 24,000 in, everyone expected us to go through to the final. But we'd lost Bellers with a hamstring injury and he was the beating heart of that side.

We were shit that night and lost 3-0. I came on after 64 minutes for Chops but were already two goals down by then and fucked. That cost Dave Jones his job and, in hindsight, I wonder if we'd approached those last few months differently and had fewer loan players in whether we would have gone up, because we blew it.

So with me thinking we'd end up in the top two, I'd double my money and, happy days, things had gone a bit pear-shaped. Not for the first time in my life, I'd failed to back a winner.

Sadly, it didn't work out for me and Clare. It was maybe too early to try a reconciliation and I hadn't really had time to change my ways. We were bickering and we both realised it wasn't going to get any better so she took Oliver and moved back to Barnsley. My son was more than 200 miles away again and I was left in a big house in the middle of nowhere on my own. That was the start of my depression.

When I did go home, I had to stay with my mum and dad which, as a 30-year-old man, didn't feel right. So Clare said: "Okay, what do you want to do about it?"

We still owned the first house we'd lived in when we got married and had been renting it out so we agreed she'd move there with Oliver and I'd take the house I owned but she'd been living in. We weren't living as husband and wife any more and it just made sense. It meant that while I was in Cardiff, my house was often empty, but I had somewhere of my own to go back to when I did go home, rather than my parents' house.

I went back to Barnsley for the summer hoping to shake off the blues. As soon as I began the journey, I started to feel a weight lift, but it all passed too quickly and it was soon time to head back to South Wales.

I spent pre-season on my own and I remember leaving Oliver and thinking about what would happen if I just didn't go back. I'm a massive home bird anyway but it was leaving my lad behind that had really killed me. I'd finally got my head around being a dad by then and was happy to make sacrifices I needed to make, but being so far away was the last thing I needed. I was sinking fast. I had that to deal with, I was apprehensive about the new manager coming in and wasn't in a good place mentally or physically.

Malky Mackay had been installed as Cardiff manager during the summer and whereas Dave Jones was laidback and just let the lads get on with it, Mackay would prove to be the total opposite – a sergeant major type who basically wanted robots who didn't answer back. Despite Bellers wanting to come back on a permanent deal, Mackay never pursued a deal with Man City and Bellers went to Liverpool instead. I could tell straight away that me and Malky weren't going to get on.

I did well in pre-season, got fit and we were playing West Ham away for the first game of the 2011/12 season. On the coach down, my roommate Mark Hudson set me up on Twitter, showed me how to use it and set up my profile. I've never been a techie in any sense of the word, so he had to do everything and then showed me how to send a tweet out if I wanted to. I'd soon learn that putting your thoughts out to the world could come back and bite you on the arse.

I was on the bench at West Ham and Mackay had brought a French kid in – Rudy Gestede – who had come on trial and was a total unknown at the time. We were drawing 0-0 at Upton Park and Mackay started preparing to bring a sub on so I thought I might get my chance – but he put Rudy on instead.

I was raging because he had put this unknown kid on before me. It told me everything I needed to know about where I stood in the pecking order – which seemed to be further down than ever. Of course, Rudy sets up the only goal of the game, we win 1-0 – the last thing I needed. Rudy was a lovely kid and I'm really happy the way things have worked out for him because he deserves it, but I was an unused sub, a teenager had gone on before me and I was wondering what was coming next. Kenny Miller – another striker – had signed for us as well, but we got on well straight away.

I remember around that time I checked my Twitter feed and saw there was one direct message from a young lad saying I'd broken his dad's arm when Preston had played Cardiff at Deepdale. I tweeted him back saying how sorry I was. He came back saying not to worry about it as they'd got a new kitchen and a holiday out of it! Cardiff's insurance must have covered it or something and I'd seemingly made a good impression on one Cardiff supporter. It turned out he might have been the only one by the time I'd finished.

Mackay played a second string for our League Cup game against Oxford United the following Tuesday, but I wasn't even on the bench for our next matches against Bristol City or our home game against Brighton, which we lost 3-1.

I thought I'd give Twitter a whirl for a laugh. I watched the game from the stands and after the match, I tweeted: "Does anyone need a gardener? Looking for work." I'd only been on Twitter for a short while and I'd gained a few hundred followers already. A few Cardiff fans replied to the tweet asking things like: "What are you fucking moaning at?" saying I was being well paid and so on. I replied, telling them it wasn't about that, I just wanted to play football.

The following Friday, Malky calls me into his office and throws a newspaper down on his desk. "What the fuck is that?" I looked at it and – I think it was The Sun – it had a headline

'Anyone looking for a gardener?' He said: "What have I told you lot about Twitter and social media?"

I had to think fast and told him I'd only been on it a few days and that I thought I'd been messaging one of my mates on it – knowing full well I hadn't. He just shook his head and said: "That's not good enough." We left it at that.

So now not only did he think I'm shit, I've also pissed him off for good measure. I wasn't involved in the next match against Burnley so I wasn't getting a sniff of the first-team but I got a run-out in our next match against Huddersfield Town in the League Cup. I did okay, scored after 17 minutes and we won 5-3 after extra-time, though I'd gone off after about an hour because I wasn't match fit.

We were away at Portsmouth at the weekend but I wasn't included again, and I was getting severely pissed off. I was missing Oliver, I was lonely living in a family house, my head wasn't right and things were building up.

I started to do something I'd never really done in my career before and became a bit of a negative influence around the club. On one particular day, I was doing some stretches with Kenny Miller on the training ground and I said to him: "They're all fucking snakes, you know." I was talking about Malky's coaching staff, none of whom I trusted.

Kenny said: "Yeah, I know. All fucking snakes." They were

always going back to Malky if anything happened, snitching on the lads, so I didn't have any time for any of them. What I hadn't realised was the fitness coach had been in earshot and when I left, Malky pulled Kenny in.

"What's all this about you and Parky calling all my staff snakes?"

Kenny said: "Well the fitness coach has obviously heard us talking, it's got back to you, so they clearly are all snakes."

If Malky hated me before, he despised me now. I'm a celebrity, get me out of here…

13

THE CURSE OF
JON PARKIN

In my second game away to Leyton Orient, I scored in a 3-1 win. The fans accepted me straight away and from their point of-view, they were getting a Championship striker for peanuts. That was until they saw me play and saw I could barely move!

I was out shopping when Tim called me to say Doncaster Rovers wanted to take me on a month's loan, which was the best news I'd had in a long while. Sean O'Driscoll was the manager, so I said: "Yep, get me home."

Chris Brown, my former housemate at Preston, was at Doncaster. He'd moved there the previous July and I'd told him he could stay at my house in Barnsley for a while as I was away a fair bit. Whenever I did go back, it had been good to have Chris as company.

I travelled down to Doncaster the next day and trained for the first time on the Thursday and really enjoyed it. It was great to be near home and I was looking forward to getting a few games under my belt again. Doncaster were struggling in the Championship but they had a good bunch of lads and it felt like a bit of a weight had lifted because I'd be able to see Oliver four or five days a week and live back home.

But like the kiss of death, I turned up for training on Friday and was told Sean O'Driscoll had been dismissed! I'd got some managers sacked in my time but never without playing first and certainly never within 48 hours.

The club didn't hang around. They brought in agent Willie Mackay, who was employed in a sort of experimental director of football role, while Dean Saunders then came in as manager. Willie's job was to find players – and he would bring in some impressive names. I didn't think Dean was a brilliant manager but I really liked him as a bloke. He was funny and had different ways of doing things.

We beat Crystal Palace 1-0 on my debut – Doncaster's first win of the season and a first win in 20 games – and then took a point at home to Hull City the following Tuesday. I'd made a solid start to my time at the club and life with Dean Saunders was never dull.

At his first Friday session he told us we were going to have a Young v Old game and prizes would be given to the winning team's best player, the scorer of the best goal and the overall man of the match. Everyone was wondering what the prizes were going to be so we played the game and the Old won 1-0 with me scoring the only goal.

We went in for lunch and afterwards, Dean started his prize-giving ceremony. He said: "Okay, so there was only one goal scored so Parky, come up and get your golf clubs. And because you scored the goal, you get man of the match as well, so take this TV too."

It was class. Golf clubs and a TV just for doing well in training. The clubs were a bit shit but I put them and the TV in my car and drove home, happy as Larry.

He told us the prizes for next Friday's session would be even better, so the Old v Young session was even better, and we were all desperate to find out what the winners had got this time. That's when we clocked a racehorse at the training ground!

One of our coaches, Mickey Walker, who had been at the club for donkey's years and was about 70, was on the horse in full silks being led around the training ground. Dean told us the winner got a half-share in the racehorse, but we smelled a rat when his assistant, who had played in the session, won the man of the match award and a share in the horse. We backed it a few weeks later and it was crap, but fair play to Dean Saunders.

The good form continued as we won 2-1 away at Peterborough, by which time I was getting fitter every time I played. I hadn't scored yet but I was doing well and we'd taken seven points from a possible nine.

The club's new transfer model was simple. They were telling other clubs that they could send the players they didn't want there and in turn they'd get game time and Doncaster would pay a maximum of £2,000 per week wages, with the parent club making up the rest.

It made good business sense all round to me because the players would basically put themselves in the shop window and if they did okay, they might even add a few quid to their price tag and make them more sellable. Or they'd improve their fitness or get experience – whatever the case, it sounded fair enough, though I wasn't sure how it would affect me going forward.

My fourth game was against Leeds United and we were well beaten 3-0 at the Keepmoat Stadium, meaning we were still right in the shit and what would turn out to be my last game for the club was a 3-1 loss away to Portsmouth.

The terms of my loan were Doncaster were paying half my wages – about £4,000 – and at the end of the month, Saunders said he wanted me to stay on. This was great because I wanted to stay, but with the new £2,000 wage ceiling for loaned players now in place, it meant Cardiff would need to pay about £6,000 if I stayed with Doncaster. They basically told Donny to get lost.

Dean told me there was nothing he could do about it and wished me well but the moment I knew I was heading back to Cardiff, I started feeling really flat again. I knew I'd be going back to a world of shit.

I headed back to Cardiff in October and was back in the house on the Sunday before my first training session back. I went straight back into the routine of training, going to bed and staying there. The only time the cycle would break was if Huds and his wife ML invited me round for the evening. That would happen a couple of nights a week, which broke things up, but I was conscious of being around too much and becoming a pain in the arse.

I headed home whenever I got the chance and I was driving 1200 miles per week on some occasions. I had a couple of weeks' training with the first-team before Malky Mackay made me train with the youth team because of the Twitter incident and the snakes episode. I was as low as I'd ever been and if Mackay ever bawled me out for any reason, I just used to ignore him. I genuinely could not give a fuck. I was not arsed what happened and he could have fined me or sacked me for all I cared – I half-hoped he would. I wasn't even eating that much any more; it was just training and sleeping for hours on end, broken up by TV occasionally.

I've always been a bit of a clown in the dressing room but I was hardly talking to anyone, interacting or joining in the banter any more. I still hadn't realised I'd slipped into a deep depression for the first time in my life. I tried to bat it off as boredom, but it wasn't me. I didn't want to go out, I was hardly drinking – I was just miserable and constantly tired. Eventually I went to see the club doctor, Len Noakes – a sensational guy and a somebody I knew I could talk to.

I told him I was struggling and he asked me why, so he asked me what had been happening and how I felt about it all. He just listened to what I had to say, which was quite liberating on its own.

When I'd finished he told me not to worry because he'd sort it and I'd soon be feeling better. He was great, he never judged me and told me he had thought something might be wrong because I hadn't been my usual self for a while. Nobody knew about it, not even my mum and dad – they will when they read this – but that is because of the stigma mental health issues carried with them a few years back. Dr Noakes set me up with another club doctor who also talked to me and asked me what made me feel happy. I told him I felt fine as soon as I was on my way back to Barnsley, so he diagnosed me with circumstantial depression because of the situation I was in. He prescribed me some anti-depressants and after a few weeks, things started to improve.

Mackay had frozen me out of anything and everything. I never travelled or trained with the first-team and he made me do extra work with the kids. I just wanted out and he clearly wanted me out as well.

After a month spinning the wheels back at Cardiff, Tim called to say Huddersfield Town wanted me on a month's loan. I would have gone there for £100 a week at that point. Incredible. Back home and 40 minutes from my house.

The anti-depressants were kicking in but I was getting it together anyway, wasn't gambling that much and had cut right down on my drinking. All I needed was to see Oliver and play football. I'd scored my only goal of the season against Huddersfield and I must have stayed in their minds.

They wanted me to go there for two months and I honestly couldn't have been happier. Lee Clark was the manager and they had gone a club record 43 games without loss, stretching across last season in League One and this one. They had lost the play-off final against Peterborough in between, but as far as league games went, they were close to going a complete year without losing a match. Then I arrived. You can probably see what's coming…

I was like a dog with two dicks driving home and as soon as I arrived back in Barnsley, I didn't give a fuck about anything. It was like a switch had been flicked and I was back to my old self. I shook Cardiff and Malky Mackay off completely and focused on Huddersfield and my debut at Charlton.

So, 43 league games and no defeat, but one game with me in their side and we lose 2-0. How's your fucking luck? Worse still, we lost the next game, too – at home to Bournemouth. They must have thought they'd signed a right Jonah. Already this season I'd seen off Sean O'Driscoll and ended Huddersfield's greatest unbeaten run of all time. The curse of Parky had struck again.

I thought it must be a piss-take. I was dropped from the starting line-up for our next game away to Sheffield Wednesday – it wasn't a problem because I still couldn't stop smiling. We were losing 4-2 at Sheffield Wednesday but Jordan Rhodes scored twice in the last 12 minutes to earn a 4-4 and end the losing sequence. I'd only played 10 minutes or so off the bench in that game and I never played for them again, but I couldn't give a shit, which was probably wrong.

I was home and seeing Oliver every day so there was nothing that could piss me off. I still had until nearly the end of January at Huddersfield, which meant I'd be spending Christmas and New Year at home.

I knew I wouldn't be kept on at Huddersfield after the way things had gone, but they'd been exactly what I needed. I went back to the unending nightmare that was Cardiff, where I was treated like shit and training the kids again thanks to my bosom buddy Malky Mackay. But I was okay. It was nearly February, I was working my way through my contract and had by then passed halfway. I was in a much better place, had stopped taking the anti-deps and was back in control of everything.

I'd been back just over a fortnight when Tim told me Alan Knill and Chris Brass at Scunthorpe wanted to take me on loan until the end of the season.

At that stage, I think Cardiff would have taken twenty quid for me but I had a bit of history with Brass after my mud-chucking incident at York eight years before. He phoned me up, we had a quick chat about it and clearly it was all in the past so he said: "Look Parky, we're struggling. Will you come until the end of the season?"

I said: "Not a problem. I can do that."

Scunthorpe were maybe third bottom of League One, but I couldn't have cared less. It was a bit further away from Barnsley, but very commutable. Scunthorpe paid £2,000 a week – the same contribution Doncaster had offered earlier in the season that they'd flatly turned down – and Cardiff about £8,000. Funny how things changed.

Brassy asked me to come in and just do my best for them. I'd not played for two months and was completely unfit after going through the motions at Cardiff, so I said: "Look, it's going to take me a couple of games to get fit, mate," and he just laughed.

I played my first game against Rochdale and we won 1-0 and then in my second game away to Leyton Orient, I scored in a 3-1 win. The fans accepted me straight away and from their point of view, they were getting a Championship striker for peanuts – that was until they saw me play and realised I could barely move!

Cardiff, meanwhile, had reached their first ever League Cup final and would be playing Liverpool. Scunny were playing Brentford the day before so I was clear to go to the game and, as I was still a Cardiff player and had played in the first two rounds, I fancied a day out at Wembley. I got in touch with the club secretary and asked what the script was for the final regarding tickets and so on. I asked if I was invited or even allowed to go as a squad member – in fact, was I even welcome? He said he'd need to speak to the manager and get back to me. I knew where this one was heading.

Later, I got a call back from the secretary who said: "Yeah, sorry Jon you're not welcome to come. If you want any tickets, you'll have to buy them." Cheers Malky.

A few of my mates are Liverpool fans so I ended up buying tickets for them and we travelled down on the Saturday evening before the game. It was outrageous, really, but it showed how isolated I'd become under Mackay. I thought, 'Fuck him, I'm going anyway' and ended up watching the game with the Cardiff fans in the stand.

Back at Scunny, we ended up going on a bit of a run. We were safe with three or four games to go and I'd scored six goals from 13 starts so it couldn't have worked out much better for them or for me. I'd done what they had asked of me and I'd proved I could still do a job, even if it had been at League One level.

I still had a year left on my contract at Cardiff City but Tim had been speaking with their sporting director, Iain Moody, who had told him they wanted to sort things out and bring this disaster of a move to an end. It made more sense for them to pay up my final year and get me out of the building rather than keep sending me out on loan. That suited me down to the ground. I think I would have rather quit football than go back to that empty house and train with the kids again, but thankfully, we sorted a settlement out. Thank fuck, my time at Cardiff was over.

14

SLEEPING WITH THE FISHES

At Southend, one of the lads missed a penalty that I would have taken so we drew, but although I tried not to be smug, I was thinking, 'Good. You should have played me, you prick. It's not your fucking money'

I had an operation on my knee at the end of the 2011/12 season – another clear-out and my second in three years. I was without a club for two months in the summer of 2012 and wondering where my future lay. I was still only 31 so I knew I had a few years left in the tank but, as ever, the doubts crept in and I wondered if anyone would want to take me on.

Alan Knill and Chris Brass said they'd like me to go back to Scunny. I was open to it as I'd enjoyed my time there but they could only offer me £2,000 per week and while it wasn't about money – thanks to my Cardiff pay-up – it was more about what would likely happen and whether that was really for me.

Did I want a dead season at my age where there was no realistic chance of going up and probably not much chance of going down? If they finished twelfth it would be a decent year for Scunthorpe, but I didn't fancy a slog of a season, a mid-table finish and that sitting okay with everyone.

I told them I'd let them know and, in the meantime, Tim was ringing around a few clubs to see if there was any interest. I wanted a club who were going to have a real go and had ambition. One of the clubs Tim had spoken to was Fleetwood Town. He'd had a chat with their chief scout Jim McNulty, who had been at Preston North End with me.

Fleetwood had just been promoted to the Football League and their star striker Jamie Vardy had left for Leicester City. Jim said Fleetwood were going to push the boat out and had an ambitious chairman so they ticked a lot of boxes for me. I didn't know how many years I had left playing so I wanted the best I could get and it sounded as if it might be quite interesting. They were paying more than Scunthorpe had offered too, so I said to Tim: "Great, I'll go and sign for them."

I'm not sure how much manager Micky Mellon knew about me but his chief scout had recommended me and I was now a Fleetwood player. I agreed a one year deal, with an agreement that if I made 24 appearances, I got the following season as well, by which time I'd be 33 or so.

I very nearly didn't play a single game for Fleetwood – or for anyone, for that matter, ever again. I'd only been at the club a few days and we were on pre-season in Austria when I had what amounts to a 'near-death experience'. In fact, it could have ended up in a manslaughter charge with yours truly the victim!

We all went out for a white water rafting session on a lake and were split into two groups. I'd done it before so I knew what to expect and as we approached the dam to go down the rapids, I stood up ready to start paddling. As I did, Fleetwood centre-back Steve McNulty pushed me over. I sank like a stone and hit the bottom, but the current was pulling me and as I tried to swim to the surface, my leg caught under the dam and I couldn't push against the current to get it free. I started to think I might be in a bit of bother. I struggled like fuck and eventually, I shook my leg free, but I then smacked into the wall of the dam and cracked my head.

So, I'm basically drowning and dazed, but free – and I floated back up to the surface about 30 feet away from the boat. The lads said I'd been under about 10 seconds and they were starting to wonder if I'd ever come up. I clambered back on to the boat and felt like twatting McNulty with an oar, but I let it ride – mostly because I was just happy to still be alive. I didn't get as far as seeing a tunnel filled with white light, but save to say I preferred the park boating lakes over white-water rafting thereafter.

I didn't hit the ground running at Fleetwood and considering I'd been at a Championship club and they'd been in the National League the year before, in theory you could say I'd dropped two or three leagues to play for them and, in turn, they would have been expecting me to score goals. I was playing okay, but I was also replacing local hero Vardy, who had scored 34 goals in 42 games the previous season, so there was a bit of pressure to deliver. I didn't score in any of our first five matches but I was enjoying it. I was just hoping I wouldn't go on a 14 or 15 game run without a goal as I'd done before at Macclesfield and Preston.

The travelling from Barnsley was a bit of a pain but we trained at Lytham which was easier to get to, so I'd done it all before and it wasn't that much different from when I'd played for Preston.

I'd not been at Fleetwood long when I was awoken at home by a phone call from my dad. I checked the time and it was

4am so I knew it couldn't be good. He told me I needed to get to the hospital quickly because my brother had collapsed at work. Jim was four years older than me and Dad told me he was in a bad way and to get there as quickly as I could.

I jumped out of bed, got dressed and got to the hospital within about 30 minutes. My mum and dad were there when I arrived and I asked Dad what had happened. He said they'd found him unconscious at work and when the paramedics had arrived, his heart had stopped. Jim is probably fitter than me – a keen cyclist, no weight on him and generally lives a healthy lifestyle – so it was hard to fathom why this had happened. It had been totally out of the blue.

He worked nights and the only saving grace was that one of his colleagues found him and was able to alert the emergency services quickly while another staff member gave him CPR. They resuscitated his heart and kept him alive but nobody knew for sure how long he'd been unconscious for, so we weren't sure how much damage had been done.

He was in intensive care for two weeks in an induced coma. During that time we were fretting as to whether the Jim we knew and loved would be the one who woke up, or somebody else. He wasn't in view of any of the CCTV cameras so nobody knew for sure if he had been unconscious for 20 minutes or longer. He lived alone and had just been off for four days, so if it had happened then, nobody would have found him – and I'd have been ordering a new black suit.

Micky Mellon was fantastic with me and he just said to take whatever time off I needed. Luckily, after a few weeks, Jim came around and though he was a bit confused and forgetful for quite a while, he was still our Jim and would eventually make a full recovery.

He has a defib fitted in his chest now and I had to go along and have tests on my heart, but it turned out to be just one of those episodes that nobody could explain or could have predicted. It was a scary time but he was okay and I could focus on football again.

Whichever way you looked at it, Fleetwood were paying massive money for League Two and I was their marquee signing. Thankfully, my mini-drought ended when we played Morecambe away. It was a local derby and a big game for our fans and I ended up scoring a hat-trick in a 4-0 win. I then went another five games without a goal meaning I'd only scored in one match out of my first 11, but finally things clicked into place and the goals started going in.

Our results had been a bit mixed but I got a couple against Bromley and then another against Rotherham. Then, on 54 minutes, I felt my hamstring go and, based on previous strains, I knew I'd be out for four to six weeks. I'd just really got going and it was the last thing I needed.

The curse was still going well, too and I wouldn't play for Micky Mellon again as he was sacked in early December. We'd been dicked 5-1 at home by arch-rivals Blackpool and even though we were fourth, Micky was shown the door. We were all like, 'Where did that come from?'

The scans had showed it was a grade two tear and it was bad timing all round because Graham Alexander had now come in as manager. I didn't know him personally, but I'd played against him a few times and knew a lot of people who knew him because of the Preston connection. He'd played more than 400 games for them and had clocked up nearly 1,000 matches overall during an incredible career.

I started working with the physio but I have to say, he wasn't the best. I did everything I was told to do and got to the stage where I was almost ready to play. So Graham had only been in a few weeks when I started training but in my first session back, my hamstring went again.

I was back out injured for however long and I was totally pissed off. A few days passed and I decided I was going to go out on the Friday. I was having a few drinks with my mates back in Barnsley when I got a text from the physio saying I was due in on Saturday morning. I was in the swing of my night out and I was wondering what I was supposed to be doing as I could hardly move my leg. At best it could be iced and maybe have a few minutes on the bike and that was that.

I wasn't sure if the physio was trying to save his job under the new manager or what but I just texted him back saying: "Do I really have to come in, mate? Can't we just say I came in for an hour as nobody will know?"

But he didn't text me back. I wasn't going to stop my night out and thought I'd just head over in the morning anyway – except I slept in. I woke up at noon the next day and should have been at Fleetwood for 10am so I messaged the physio and told him I'd overslept, but again he didn't reply, and I started to wonder why.

So I get back in on the Monday and nobody says a thing to me. It was the same on Tuesday and the same on Wednesday. I was keeping a low profile, keeping my head down and was starting to think I'd got away with it but on Thursday, Alexander pulls me into his office and says: "What the fuck happened on Saturday?"

I said: "Look, I'm really sorry. I overslept and that's all."

He goes: "Well Martin's showed me your message."

I said I'd only been messing about and then had genuinely slept in but he asked why I'd not been in to see him for the past three days and I just said: "Well, obviously I thought it wasn't a massive problem, but now I can see it is."

He told me I was out of order and then said he was fining me a week's wages. "What do you think of that?"

Deep down I was thinking, 'Fuck you, pal.' I'd only missed an hour of icing my leg, but I said: "Okay, if I'm fined a week's wages, are we drawing a line under this and are we done?" He said that as far as he was concerned, yes. It wasn't the best start under the new manager – he'd been in eight weeks, I still hadn't played a game for him and now I'd been fined for ducking a physio session.

But things were about to get better and by the end of January, I was fit and I scored in my first three games back, which was a massive relief. But in the third of those games, away to Torquay, I felt a tweak in my hamstring again and had to come off with 38 minutes played.

It wasn't a bad one this time and I'd only be out for a fortnight, but I was starting to get wary about my agreement of making 24 league appearances to get another year at Fleetwood. I'd only made 14 so far so I needed to play regularly or else they'd be able to let me go. I was back at the end of February and didn't score for four games before getting a hat-trick away to

Accrington Stanley. I'd scored 12 in 19 League Two games so when I had been fit, I was making a decent contribution. But after scoring that hat-trick, I was then on the bench for the trip to Plymouth the following week, which I thought was more than a bit fishy, pardon the pun. I knew deep down it was all to do with the agreed appearances clause but we had half a chance of getting in the play-offs so if it was the reason, it seemed madness.

I was back in the starting line-up for a 2-0 away defeat at Barnet and I then came off the bench to help us come back and draw 2-2 with Gillingham. We then had a match on the Bank Holiday Monday at Southend United, but after we'd played Gillingham, Alexander said: "Look, Parky – I can't play you again. You're on too much money."

I'd made 22 league appearances – two short of the deal for next season being activated. We still had four weeks and five matches to play, I was the top scorer – and now they weren't going to play me?

He said: "I want you to stay next season, but we can't afford to pay the wages you're on. You're on too much and you've had too many injuries plus you'll be 32 next December."

I said: "What are you going to do then?"

He said he would have to try and sort a deal out, but that I wouldn't be travelling to Southend on Monday as there was no point. I was thinking, 'Brilliant! I can go out Sunday and enjoy Bank Holiday Monday. I suppose I was half-expecting them to do this, but I'd done alright for them and we had a chance of going up so I felt a bit let down as well.

I told Alexander to try and sort it, but it was nuts. At Southend one of the lads missed a penalty that I would have taken so we drew, but although I tried to not be smug, I was thinking, 'Good. You should have played me, you prick. It's not your fucking money.'

I didn't play again that season and of the five games I missed, we took one point out of 15 and ended up missing out on the play-offs by nine points. It served Alexander right. I hadn't played a game for nearly five weeks while they tried to sort my contract out and the chief executive and my agent were at loggerheads because Fleetwood were saying they could only offer so much, Tim was telling him that it wasn't good enough blah, blah, blah, blah.

They were going around in circles so I decided to call the chairman myself. I said: "Hello chairman, look, you were willing to pay me the wages I was on this season and I've done well for you. If I'd made two more appearances I'd have got the same deal I'd had this season and, but for injury, I would have done and we wouldn't even be having this conversation. I've been told the wages you're offering, and I'll sign for that.

Whether you tell the manager or not is up to you, but if he wants me to stay, I'll sign for what you're offering."

It wasn't outrageous by any means and the chairman just said: "Yeah, I'll do that." So, after all the toing and froing, it took me less than ten minutes to agree a new, one-year deal. I'd taken a pay cut, but happy days, I had a club and I could now look ahead to the summer knowing that I'd still be playing league football going into my 33rd year.

15

THE CODFATHER

He said there was a pie shop he knew of – sounded like my sort of establishment – and I told him to get his foot down. Thank fuck when we got there it was open, so I got a couple of pies and then went looking for yet another taxi. Those two pies had cost me more than €80!

I had a decent pre-season as we went into 2013/14 and scored a few goals in the friendlies we played, but by the opening day, I wasn't in the team. In fact, I didn't play in any of our first five games.

I was wondering what was going on so I decided to go and see Graham Alexander. Maybe it was because I'd negotiated my own deal with the chairman and he'd seen his arse about it, or maybe he hadn't really wanted me to sign another year after all.

I went in and asked what the issue was and he told me in his opinion I wasn't fit enough. I said: "Okay, but the only way I'll get fitter is by playing matches."

He disagreed and said he thought I could get fit on the training ground. I said: "You might have been able to do that when you were playing your thousand games, but I just can't. I need to play matches."

The team was doing okay, don't get me wrong, but having just agreed a new contract based on the premise I'd be playing, and we'd be going for it, it wasn't quite panning out like that. I was back in the team for the last game of August and seemingly back in favour for a while, going on a run of four goals in six games. But I wasn't 100 per cent sure where I stood with the manager.

We had a Saturday night out in Poulton-le-Fylde where the chairman owned some luxury flats called The Breck, so we decided to make that our base for the night. We went out, had a good few beers and stayed at the flat overnight. It had a wet room bathroom and during the night, someone had got up and taken a piss on the floor. On the Monday, Alexander pulled me to one side and asked if we'd been out on Saturday. I said yeah and then he said: "Did you stay at The Breck?" I told him we had, and he said: "Well someone has been pissing on the bathroom floor."

I honestly didn't know if it had been me or not but he said the chairman was raging and that I needed to phone him straight away. "Was it you?" he asked. I said I really didn't know but I'd take the blame for it anyway and call the chairman. So I did. He answered: "Is that piss-pot Parkin?"

"Hello chairman. Look, I'm not 100 per cent sure if it was me but I'll take the blame for it and just wanted to ring and apologise for what went off at The Breck."

He said. "Okay, just order some flowers for the cleaners and we'll leave it at that."

I'd half-thought I might get another fine, but he was good as gold in fairness. He was a bit of a lad too and enjoyed a drink, so I think he could sympathise with how inexplicable things sometimes just happen.

Back on the pitch, we'd begun playing 4-5-1 and we'd started to struggle. It was David Ball who got the nod as the lone striker more often than not, but teams soon worked us out, would drop off us and when the ball was played to Bally, who was only five feet eight inches, it was coming straight back at us. The formation just didn't suit the players we had, and I was telling the lads after games we needed to switch back to 4-4-2. We'd taken just one point from a possible 15 and just before Christmas, Alexander pulls me to one side and said: "I hear you think we should go back to 4-4-2?"

I said: "Yeah, I do."

"Why?"

So I said: "Teams have worked us out, they drop off and when we pump the ball forward it's coming straight back off Bally."

He had a bit of a go at me and suggested I was being disruptive, so I just said: "Look, you're the boss but I think we'd just do better with 4-4-2."

We played Morecambe on Boxing Day and were crap. We never looked like scoring and I came on as a second-half sub. We went back into the dressing room and Alexander said to us all: "Right, over to you. What do you think?"

So I said: "I think we need to play 4-4-2," and a few of the lads said the same thing and he just nodded. He took it on board and we were due to play Wycombe and he was going to go from one extreme to the other and play 4-3-3 that day – but the game was called off not long before kick-off due to a frozen pitch.

Our next game was Accrington at home. This time he played 4-4-2, I scored and we won 3-1 – the first time in three months we'd scored more than two goals in a game. I had a bit of a smug grin on my face after that and we went on to win four games out of the next five, I scored three goals and he gets manager of the month! I think I was up for player of the month, too, so it was a bit like, 'fuck you.'

We were back on track and were up around the play-offs going into March. With seven games left, we were playing Exeter away. I'd noticed by now that if things weren't going well for the team, Alexander would always take me off, no matter how I was playing.

We were losing 3-0 at Exeter and I'd already told a few of the lads that I'd be taken off if we hadn't scored by the hour-mark – and sure enough, that's pretty much what happened. Our relationship was strained to say the least and I sat down and was thrashing my boots around and generally making a bit of scene. I said: "This is shit. I fucking knew this was going to happen."

Alexander didn't say anything but we had a game the following Tuesday and he'd not named the team so I arrived at the ground for the rearranged game against Wycombe and went into the dressing room where I saw my shirt among the subs' shirts.

So he names the team and I'm sub and I'd had enough. I went into a proper strop. I didn't say anything to begin with but I never moved and was silent, so it wasn't difficult to tell how pissed off I was. By 6.50pm all the lads were getting changed, ready to warm up and I was still sat there, fully dressed, sulking in the corner.

Alexander says: "Parky," and nodded for me to follow him back to his office. I was stamping my feet behind him and as I closed the door behind me, he just said: "Frustrated?"

"Frustrated? Are you taking the piss? I fucking knew that would happen at Exeter. When we played Dagenham, you fetched [Mikael] Mandron on and at Exeter, it's happened again and now I'm not even playing."

I'd gone by this stage and I honestly thought I was going to hit him. I put my hands in my pockets just in case, but they were shaking, and I think he could sense I was on the edge.

"I just don't think you can play two games in three days," he said.

"What a load of shit that is," I replied.

He asked me if I wanted to be on the bench or not, so I said I didn't want to be on the bench, but I would do it. He told me I'd better go and get changed, but that remains the closest I ever came to hitting a manager. I didn't come on and I didn't start another game until our last match of the season. Iain

Hume had come in and is a great lad who I love to bits, but he'd only scored one in 11 games and I thought I should have been starting games.

We were in fourth going into the final day – and would finish fourth no matter what. We were away to Chesterfield who were already promoted and could seal the title if they won against us. It was a red-hot day, a full house and Alexander picked everyone who hadn't been playing ahead of the play-off semi-finals, which included me.

By half time, we were winning 1 0 and I said in the dressing room before the manager came in: "This wasn't supposed to happen was it?" A few of us were laughing and I said: "I bet he's out there now scratching his head."

I don't think us doing so well had come into the equation and we were potentially giving him a problem for the play-offs. As it was, Chesterfield scored on 51 minutes to make it 1-1 and then Gary Roberts scored again for them on 55 so obviously, the atmosphere was one of celebration and if things stayed the same, they were champions.

We had nothing to lose and were still well in the game so I was thinking that we would probably throw caution to the wind and go for an equaliser. They were playing keep-ball and their fans were giving it 'Ole!' every time they made a pass.

Then the board goes up on 73 minutes – but this time it's

not me. Josh Morris, my strike partner, is taken off and Matty Hughes came on but goes in midfield. I was raging because we might as well have brought two more forwards on and tried to get a goal – what did it matter if we lost 3-1 or 4-1 trying? They played out the last few minutes and won the game 2-1 so obviously their fans pour onto the pitch, they're champions and we all tried to make our way back to the dressing room as quickly as we could.

The fans were rubbing my head, taking the piss and, finally, we made it back in and everyone was just sat there, quiet so I said: "That was fucking shit!"

Alexander said: "What?"

"You know what. You just hung us out to dry there. Losing 2-1 and you go with just one up front? That's fucking crap, that."

He asked what I meant, and I said: "You know exactly what you've done. You changed the formation and half-chucked it. People have paid good money to watch that.'"

He asked whether I'd rather we'd lost by three or four goals going into the play-offs the following Friday, so I said: "Yeah, I would. I'd rather do that trying to get back in the game. Besides, you know who is playing on Friday and none of us will be involved anyway."

Meanwhile, Ryan Cresswell, who I used to travel over with

and who, like the rest of us, didn't play that often, had been on the other side of the pitch when the crowd came on. He flung the dressing room door open and said: "Fucking shit, that!"

He kicked the physio bed and then said to Alexander: "You fucking hung us out to dry!" It sounded as though we'd set it up in the car the day before, but we hadn't. Everything had just about died down by that point and Alexander said: "Don't you start, we've just had that."

I didn't play in the semi-final first leg, but we beat York City 1-0 at Bootham Crescent and I played the last 25 minutes of the return leg which ended 0-0.

We'd made it to the play-off final and what would very likely be my final appearance for Fleetwood Town could come at Wembley – though I knew I wouldn't be starting with what had gone on previously. I came on with 74 minutes gone and we scored on 75, won the game 1-0 and were promoted to League One.

We went back to the hotel and celebrated and then we were meant to fly out to Vegas but because of the play-offs, one of the lads had his wedding in Scotland the following Saturday while we'd have been in the States, so we settled on a few days in Magaluf instead. About 12 of us headed out and we were back on Friday in time to go to the wedding.

I travelled up to Edinburgh and was sharing my hotel room

with Fleetwood team-mate Matty Blair. We'd been to the wedding and the evening reception afterwards. I was absolutely starving so I called room service only to find there wasn't any for some reason.

It was the early hours but being Edinburgh, I thought there would be somewhere open. I went out on to the main high street and flagged a rickshaw down. I asked the guy if there was a Chinatown nearby and he said there was. I told him to take me there and not to spare the horses.

It took an age. It must have been on the other side of the city and when we finally got there he told me the fare was £50, so I paid him and started walking around Chinatown only to discover it was shut. It was 4am and I hadn't a clue where I was so I managed to hail a taxi and I asked the driver if there was anywhere I could get anything to eat.

He said there was a pie shop he knew of – sounded like my sort of establishment – and I told him to get his foot down. Thank fuck when we got there it was open, so I got a couple of pies and then went looking for yet another taxi to take me back to the hotel. By the time I got back, those two pies had cost me more than £80.

We drove back the next day and, on the journey, I got a call from Graham Alexander who said: "Parky, just thought I'd let you know we won't be offering you a new deal next season."

I just said: "Right, bye," quickly and hung up.

I knew they weren't going to ask me to stay on anyway but he was well aware I'd been at the wedding and that I'd probably be on my way home when he called, so I thought it was a bit shit if I'm honest. An arranged meeting and him telling me face to face would have been the decent thing to do but I just felt he'd been a bit of a shit bag about the whole episode.

So, aged 32, I was again looking for a new club and, as ever, I was wondering whether I'd get one or not, knowing that every year that passed brought the end of my career a little bit closer.

16

WHERE THE F*** IS FOREST GREEN?

> We gave one of the apprentices £50 a month to make us unlimited teas! Any one of us could be in our beds, fancy a brew and just text the kid who would have to go up three flights of stairs to bring it to us. He didn't mind, and we didn't mind paying him to do it. Kept him fit, too

My agent told me Chesterfield were interested and as far as I was concerned, that would have been the perfect move for me.

They'd just gone up to League One as champions and they played good, attacking football with Paul Cook as their manager. It wasn't a hard decision to make and I told Tim to crack on and get it sorted.

Everyone was back in training and I still didn't have a club but Chesterfield had played a friendly, drawn 1-1 with Buxton and I think the chief executive Chris Turner must have thought they didn't have enough experience or firepower for League One. He called Tim to say they wanted to sign me.

So I went to meet him on a Friday in early July, had a chat with Paul Cook and his assistant, where he told me they didn't have much money to play with but they'd be happy to have me aboard. We sorted an agreeable contract out and they said they'd have to finalise the paperwork and I'd come back in on Monday morning to sign.

It was a weight off. I'd be a Chesterfield player on Monday and even though I'd been binned off by Fleetwood, I'd still end up in League One with arguably a better team. That would be two fingers up to Graham Alexander.

I took Oliver swimming on the Sunday and had a great time, got back home and saw I had two missed calls from Tim and a text message saying Paul Cook had pulled the plug. Here we go…

So I called Tim to find out what had happened and he told me Cook had changed his mind. He'd decided to go with youth instead of experience and that they were retracting their offer of a one-year contract. He'd pulled the plug and there I was, two weeks into pre-season and still without a club. Cheers, Cooky! I was now really struggling and thought maybe this was the end.

I went to a local music festival, had a few beers and tried not to think about it too much. Tim was working in the background as he always did. Of all the career decisions I'd made, having him as my agent was one of the best. He had his work cut out having me as his client, but he was always positive, supportive and had my back.

Of course, it wasn't long before he'd come up with another possible move – though it would mean dropping out of the Football League for the first time. Apparently, Adrian Pennock at Forest Green had been on and wanted to sign me and was offering a decent contract. I said to Tim: "Fantastic. Just one thing though – where the fuck is Forest Green?"

Tim told me it was just south of Cheltenham in Gloucestershire and I knew I'd need to move if I wanted to join them. It goes without saying that leaving Oliver was the last thing I wanted to do but I was in the last throes of my playing career and needed a club, so it wouldn't be forever.

I travelled down, had talks with the manager and the owner and it turned out the contract they were offering as a National League club was better than the one League One deal Chesterfield had offered. They had ambition too, and the owner was determined to take them into League Two. They'd sold the club and their ambition to me in about five minutes.

They'd offered me a one-year contract and if I played 30 games, I'd get the year after as well, which was perfect. I signed for them and officially became a non-league player for the first time in my career, but Forest Green were a well-run, ambitious family club and probably better than the majority of League Two clubs and a fair few League One sides as well.

During the time I'd had no club, I'd been training with Lincoln City as their manager Gary Simpson had said I'd be fine to go in whenever I needed. They'd tried to sign me a few times over the years. I needed to keep as fit as I could in case anybody signed me so I wasn't in bad shape by my lofty pre-season standards by the time I headed to Forest Green.

The club was based at Nailsworth in the Cotswolds, which was a lovely place with a population of less than 8,000. I knew I'd need to start looking around for somewhere to live and asked at the club if anyone had any ideas. Adrian Pennock said the club had a hostel if I wanted to stay there and I was like: "A hostel? I'm 33, not 17. Thanks, but no thanks."

So I moved into a hotel when I first moved down and it didn't take me long to feel bored shitless. I decided to go and have a look at the hostel – how bad could it be? It turned out to be like a four-storey office block owned by the chairman with an eating area, five bedrooms on the first floor and five on the second, with the top floor a sort of open plan living room and kitchen.

I didn't want to be on my own again after my experiences at Cardiff so I thought, 'Fuck it, I'll move in.' It was the best decision I could have made. I was like a 33-year-old student. It was incredible. There were a few other lads staying there who played for the club at various age levels. Our day would be made up of training, then maybe going into town for something to eat and then just hanging out with the guys.

There were some great lads there and we could play darts, pool, watch TV and we even had one of the apprentices staying there who we gave £50 a month to make us unlimited teas! Any one of us could be in our beds, fancy a brew and just text the kid who would have to go up three flights of stairs to bring it to us. He didn't mind, and we didn't mind paying him to do it. Kept him fit, too.

Wherever we played, I always had my car brought up behind the team coach and after the match, I'd drive home to see

Oliver. I was on the road a lot, but I didn't mind. Not for the first time in my career, I didn't make the best of starts and had scored just two goals in my first eight games, but we were going well and were up around the play-offs.

By mid-October I'd scored six goals in 16 games but probably wasn't doing as well as I should have been given my experience. It was only a few years ago that I was with a Premier League club and Forest Green had a right to think I should have been doing better at National League level.

I then went on a run of eight games without scoring between October and early December – what was it with me and autumn? What had looked an average return now looked a bit shit with six goals in 24 matches.

I finally ended my latest autumnal drought with a goal against Woking in early December and, shortly after, we had a sort of team bonding day out at a German market in Birmingham and stayed overnight. I was driving back the next day and I got a phone call from the gaffer. He said: "Hi Parky, I need a word with you."

I told him I had two per cent battery and that I'd call him the minute I got back to the hostel. I was wondering what I'd done all the way home, and when I got there, I put my mobile on charge and phoned him back. It couldn't be good and while it wasn't bad, it wasn't really what I'd wanted to hear.

He said: "Gillingham have been on the phone. Peter Taylor wants you to go there on loan. I'm after their striker, Danny Kedwell. Taylor said the only chance is if you go the other way. What do you think?"

They were in League One at the time, so it would have been a decent move, but for me there was more to it than that. If he was asking me, it meant he was fine with losing me. So I put him on the spot and said: "Do you not want me then?"

"No, no… it's not like that."

I said: "Well it is like that. You don't want me, do you?"

He paused and then said: "Well, you've not done as well as we thought you would, Parky…"

I told him I totally agreed with that. He asked me whether I'd be interested in going to Gillingham or not, but I needed him to tell me he didn't want me any more. I pressed again.

"So gaffer, do you not want me then or what?"

He wouldn't say it, but I knew he wasn't having me. I was on good money but I hadn't scored half the goals I should have. So while I understood it, I still needed him to admit he didn't want me to play for him any more.

Going to League One was a good move for me but I was already only about 10 games from guaranteeing another season at Forest Green, where I was settled and happy. Plus, if I went to Gillingham on loan and Kedwell did well in my absence, I'd be coming back with no contract in place for next season and nowhere to go. It just wasn't worth the gamble – plus it meant playing for a team in Kent which was a long way further south than Forest Green.

Had my year been guaranteed already, I might have thought about it but I just told Ady I'd have a think about it and left it at that. I'd already made my mind up, though. I talked with Tim and told him I wasn't doing it and he agreed.

It turned out I was right. We lost our next two games and I was by then on seven goals from 28 games, but I was about to hit one of my best scoring patches of my career and in the next 11 games I scored 12 goals. Suddenly it was 19 from 39 games and things looked a lot better – plus I was now guaranteed another year with Forest Green.

It was all about getting as much as I could out of my career at that stage because I knew I was getting close to a point when the offers would dry up and/or I just couldn't do it any more.

I can't explain why things started going for me, but throughout my career I'd enjoyed these patches when everything I hit seemed to go in. I suppose there are many strikers who are the same. It didn't exactly end either and I continued scoring towards the end of the season.

One of my goals – at home to Macclesfield Town of all clubs – grabbed a few headlines too, but this time for the right reasons. The ball came to me on the halfway line and I just thought I'd have a go. I hit it up high with power and fuck me, it actually went in! The fans and everyone else around me just went mad but I hardly celebrated it.

To me, it wasn't a special goal because it was nothing more than a big hoof towards the net. If you can hit a ball 50 yards, anyone can do it. I'd tried it about 300 times over the years but, as I say, there was no great technique in it – the only thing that stood out was the distance.

I honestly got more pleasure from goals like the last minute winner for Preston against Birmingham or my chest and volley against Leeds United when I was at Hull – until I saw that linesman's flag and they disallowed it!

It all went a bit nuts for a few days after that with the goal getting played over social media and what not, but I wouldn't even class it in my top ten goals.

I finished the season as top scorer with 30 goals from 52 games and I couldn't have asked for much more. It had been a season of two halves. I suppose if I'd ended up with 10 goals, I might have questioned whether I could still do it, but I'd proved I wasn't ready for the scrapyard just yet – I was on the way there, but there were still a couple of stops before I reached my destination. There was life in the old dog yet.

The Forest Green fans were great, but they are a strange

bunch – and I don't mean that in a bad way. There are quite a few older fans who must have followed the club for a good few years and they were the sort who applauded the away teams and their supporters. Quaint, I suppose you'd call them.

It was different, that's for sure, but we'd done well that season and finished in the play-offs, which was the least that was expected given the amount that had been spent on the squad. But then we came up against a smart Bristol Rovers side who just had too much for us.

They were experienced, had a strong squad who knew how to get the job done and had gone all out to get back into the Football League so fair play to them. We lost the first leg 1-0 at home and the second leg 2-0 at their place.

During my first year in the Cotswolds, I also struck up one of the most unlikely friendships of my career. Best-selling author Jilly Cooper often came to watch Forest Green and I remember getting a message after one game to meet her as she had a project she wanted me to help her with.

She invited me to her house to pick my brains about a football book she was writing. We ended up getting along like a house on fire and we have been best friends ever since.

We regularly keep in touch and I've been to a few of her summer parties, plus she sends me Christmas cards and a Valentine's Day card every year! Who'd have thought, eh?

17

NEXT STOP NEWPORT

I was faced with another new manager after just six weeks or so as a Newport County player. Everyone in football knows what he's like as a manager. My first reaction to his appointment was literally, 'Oh, for fuck's sake'

I enjoyed my summer back in Barnsley, saw plenty of Oliver and returned for my eighteenth season as a professional footballer. It was all a long way from when I'd been about to jack it all in as a kid. My dad, Paula and Tim – among others – had been right to talk me out of becoming a nursery nurse.

I'd also met Lucy by this stage. She lived in Swindon and we just sort of hit it off from the word go. She was working as an air stewardess at RAF Brize Norton and was employed by a company who sublet their planes to fly Air Force personnel around the world. She then moved into the office as a PA for the seven company directors. We just got along like a house on fire from the start.

I'd had the same clause put in my new contract with Forest Green that if I played so many games, it activated the option for me to have another season with them. I think I needed to play about 35 games to trigger a new deal and I was determined to make sure I did.

We began the season well and I scored the winner on the opening-day win at Altrincham. Then we beat Welling and Lincoln, though I was sub for the latter and on the bench again for our next game at Kidderminster.

Being sub meant that I got to warm up by the corner flag in front of some of the home fans and one in particular was giving me dog's abuse. He was pissed and probably in his early twenties. As I did my stretches, he leaned over the wall and said: "Oi, Parkin! Your mum takes it up the arse!"

I was like: "Oh, right?"

He said: "Yeah, she fucking loves it up the arse."

So I just said: "Okay, thanks – I'll tell my dad because I'm not sure if she knows she likes it up her arse than much or not. Don't worry, I'll be sure to let my dad know."

I got the call to go back to the bench because I was going on and we had a free-kick. It came into the box and I got there before the keeper and headed into the net. First touch. I was running back giving v-signs to that corner of their fans, it was like, 'Fuck off!'

That's always the best way to answer and if you're worrying about my mum reading this, don't. Trust me, she'll be sat there with a smile on her face while my dad just shakes his head!

So we were off to a flyer, winning the first seven matches. Overall, I didn't make the best of starts with just four goals in the first 12 games and half of me was thinking, 'Here we go again…' As we went along, I'd scored 13 goals in the first 32 games, but though I'd not been as prolific as the previous season, we were in with a good chance of promotion.

I wasn't panicking too much. I'd almost played the set amount needed for a third year at the club when Ady Pennock pulled me to one side and asked me to have a walk around the pitch with him. He said: "Would you consider taking out that additional year clause out for next season?"

I said: "Are you taking the piss?"

"What do you mean?" he asked.

"You're talking the piss, aren't you? I'm not being funny

but why would I take a year's guaranteed salary out of my contract?"

He said: "I want you to stay, but I want to reduce your terms."

I just shook my head. "I can't actually believe you've asked me that. If I was an 18-year-old kid, maybe I could understand it, but I'm 34. Why would I do that?"

He told me he was going to offer me a coaching role and all that next season, but I just told him I didn't give a fuck and it wasn't going to happen. I said if he didn't want to play me because I'd reach the activation point, then don't play me – but said if he did go down that road, he'd have a problem.

I asked him if he'd toss off a year out of his contract if he was asked to and he couldn't give me a coherent answer. I told him we weren't kids and to be realistic. That was the end of it. As it was, he didn't see his arse, kept picking me and I passed the agreed games amount to trigger a third year.

I didn't find the net in any of our last 12 games so I'm not sure how much that conversation affected me, and we weren't in the best of form as a team. It was the worst time to have a blip and before our last game of the season against Dover, Pennock was sacked. I had to wonder whether he hadn't brought it on himself, because his timing with me had been ridiculous.

We'd been second for a while and had had a chance of

catching leaders Cheltenham, but we hadn't won in six games, drawing five of them, and Cheltenham had pulled clear and won the league. We were well clear in second, but it was still a bit of a shock that Ady had been shown the door at that stage of the season.

But he was gone and that was that. The chairman put Scott Bartlett, our youth team manager, in charge for the play-offs. Scott asked me and secretary James Mooney to help him do it. Because I was coaching and my lack of form, we decided I wasn't going to start any of the play-off games, which I was more than fine with. The lads did well and won our two-legged semi against Dover to set up a final against Grimsby Town at Wembley.

I was on the bench with Scotty, but in the meantime the chairman had brought in Mark Cooper for the season after. We'd seen him loitering about the place for a week or so in between, but the message had been that he wouldn't start until next season.

We were doing well against Grimsby but conceded two just before half-time to go in 2-0 down at the break. We went in the dressing room and Cooper came in and said: "Right, we're going to change things." He said I was going on and made a few tactical alterations as we tried to save the game.

I missed a sitter before Keanu Marsh-Brown halved the

deficit on the hour, so we were right back in it. I was still raging about the chance I'd missed and when another opportunity came my way, I accidentally cleared out their centre-half by trying too hard.

It looked even worse on the TV replays, but the ref hadn't seen it, though it wouldn't be the last I heard of it. It wasn't going well and though we had our chances, they scored a third in the 89th minute. There was no way back.

For the icing on the cake, a few days later I was informed I had received a retrospective three-match ban for violent conduct based on the video evidence submitted to the FA, meaning I'd be banned for the first three games of the 2016/17 season. Not ideal to say the least, especially with a new manager in place who everyone would be looking to impress.

That was in the future, though. I was looking forward to the summer which would be spent with Lucy as well as seeing Oliver as much as I could. It was pretty uneventful in comparison to summers past. I did still rest, relax and enjoy myself, but nothing wild. Those days were gone.

I was never sure of which season would be my last. Though I knew it was on the horizon, I had secured another season with Forest Green and didn't have to stress too much in that respect.

Then about a week before pre-season started, I got a call

from the new sporting director who'd come in. He said: "Hello Jon. We've been discussing the season ahead and the direction we're looking to go, and we've decided we'd like to offer you a pay-up."

I was like: "Right, happy days. Let's see if we can get it sorted but don't take the piss because if you do, there's no point in us even talking."

They didn't give me a reason or anything, but it was obvious Mark Cooper didn't want me, so I let Tim negotiate with the club and they came to an agreeable figure to buy me out of my final year. It took a couple of weeks to sort out and I asked if I could still train with the lads and do a pre-season to get fit while I looked for another club. He said that wasn't a problem which, in fairness, he didn't have to do. I was glad it was an amicable parting because I'd enjoyed my time there.

I can only think Mark Cooper didn't want an experienced player in the dressing room who would have an opinion. It's fair to say I'd probably have had one or two things to say during the course of the season.

I trained with Forest Green and built my fitness up, waiting for something to happen. Soon I got a call from Barrow asking me to go and have a chat with their manager, Paul Cox. It sounded interesting.

Barrow trained in Manchester, which would have been ideal.

They were owned by a Texan who was putting some money into the club and after being impressed with what they'd had to say, I ended up agreeing a contract in principle.

I then got a call from Danny Coles, a guy who I'd played with at Hull and Forest Green but had now started doing a bit of agency work. He said Warren Feeney had been on and wanted to know if I fancied going to Newport County. It would only be an hour and 15 minutes from Lucy's house in Swindon so I said I'd give him a call.

Feeno was a top guy and it didn't take me long to decide I would give it a go. He wanted me to go to Poland with Newport for a week, but I told him I didn't fancy that, especially as I wouldn't be signing until the following week and if I got injured, I'd be back to square one.

I had been due to sign for Barrow on the Monday but when Feeno got back from Poland, he asked me to come over and sign the contract on the Sunday before, which I did. I texted Paul Cox and let him know that I had signed for Newport County, saying it was League Two, better money and that I was at a stage of my career when I needed to take the best offer available and that I was sorry about the way it had panned out.

They were fine about it and anyone would have probably done the same thing. They wished me well and that was the end of it.

Lucy said I could move in with her as Swindon wasn't a million miles from Newport. It was perfect as it was the next logical step for us anyway, and it gave me the bit of stability that had been missing for a while.

Lucy was as good as gold, but it was tough for her because as soon as I'd finished matches, I'd drive home to see Oliver, so we rarely had a weekend or any amount of time together. She missed out on nights out, meals and just being together and I know it wasn't easy. It was basically just: "Bye, see you tomorrow night," and then I'd be off. She'd occasionally come back to Barnsley with me, but it was a long journey for just one day. But she stuck by me all the time I was at Forest Green and she would do the same while I was with Newport.

I was still suspended for the first three games of the 2016/17 season for my sending off at Wembley and so made my debut against Luton Town, coming on as a sub and not really affecting the game in a 2-1 defeat at Kenilworth Road.

My first start was away to one of my (many) former clubs and it was also where I scored my first goal in a 2-2 draw with Hartlepool – an outrageous volley that pinged into my chest and went into the air before I thumped it home from 25 yards or so to silence one or two dissenters in the home end. I managed another couple against Cheltenham on my full home debut – another 2-2 draw, but we'd been dicked 4-1 in between and weren't doing that well.

I was starting to get into it and we weren't as bad as our form suggested – we were in most of the games but weren't getting the rub of the green. Feeno had been on thin ice because of how the previous season had ended and had needed a good start. We weren't that far away but the board decided to sack him and I was sorry to see him go.

I was faced with another new manager after just six weeks or so as a Newport County player. If I could have chosen just one manager I didn't want to play under at that stage – apart from Phil Brown or Steve Parkin – it would have been Graham Westley. I knew him from my Preston days and everyone in football knows what he is like as a manager. For me, it couldn't have been any worse.

I knew he liked keeping his players in all day, the training was stupidly ridiculous, and he'd have us watching videos that could send a glass eye to sleep for hours on end. While I don't mind working hard, this was another level.

He'd had success at Stevenage using similar methods but he'd brought in lads who were suited to his style – they'd signed for him, knew what he was about and bought into his style and work ethic. My first reaction to his appointment was literally, 'Oh for fuck's sake.'

He came to watch us draw 0-0 at Colchester and our first day with him was the following Monday. I was 34 going on 35 and needed an easy day on Monday if I'd played on the Saturday, so Westley's first session almost killed me.

It wasn't just me, everyone was saying the same thing. In the first fortnight we had eight muscle injuries, which was almost unheard of. The Newport physio who had been there prior to Westley's arrival quit saying it was madness. Even worse, we had a running track around the pitch – it was like a dream for our new boss.

But I had no issue with him as a person – he was good as gold with me and a genuinely nice guy. It was just like oil and water in terms of what I needed to do to stay operational and what he wanted from his players.

I didn't agree with his methods and he was probably well aware of it, so he asked me to go for a coffee with him, which I did. He said: "Look Parky, if you get on board with this, I'll look after you and you'll be able to play for another five years."

Five years? I wasn't sure I was going to last another five weeks and I suppose that was the straw that broke the donkey's back. It was going to be his way or the highway.

I played against Yeovil Town in his first game as manager and then scored another outrageous volley at home to Plymouth the week after. I think I'd proved I was maybe better than Westley had first thought I was going to be, but the price for that goal was tweaking my hamstring about five minutes later. It would turn out to be my last meaningful act in a Newport County shirt.

It rains a lot in South Wales, the pitches are heavy and with Westley's training I'd managed to last all of two weeks. I was out for six weeks minimum and while I was recovering, I was watching what the lads were having to do and I just thought, 'Nah, this isn't for me.' I just physically couldn't do it and with my trips home to see Oliver thrown in, it was impossible. What's more, I didn't want to do it.

At some stage while I was out, Eastleigh contacted Newport to see if I'd be interested in signing for them. They were throwing ridiculous money at it – obscene for National League wages – so I immediately thought this could be my last decent pay day.

Graham Westley said I was fine to talk to them if I wanted to and their assistant manager really wanted me in, but manager Ronnie Moore was a bit undecided. It got to the stage where they said they wanted me to sign so I told them, fine – sort the contract out with Tim and I'd come down and play for them.

It turned out they only wanted to take over my contract

from Newport, but I wasn't interested in that. I knew what they'd been paying other players, so it felt like they'd be getting me on the cheap. I said no to that and told them what I was looking for. It was nowhere near what some of their lads were on and wasn't greedy.

But they didn't want to pay me any more than I was already on, so I said: "What's the point of me dropping down a league and moving further away from my lad just to be paid the same as I was on at Newport?"

I said 'thanks but no thanks' and focused on recovering from my hamstring injury instead. I was nearing a full recovery when I fell out properly with Westley and pretty much ended my time with the club.

The youth team physio had been promoted when the original physio had walked and I felt Westley knew he was scared of him because he was young and new to the first-team role. Instead of speaking up and saying some of the training was actually injuring our players, he just did what he was told. It was understandable as he was just making his way.

I'd reached the stage of my recovery where I needed to start sprinting to test my hamstring out and on this particular morning, Mike Flynn, Westley's assistant, came over and said: "You need to do 10 laps of the running track as fast as you can. The gaffer wants you to do it."

I said: "What? That's bollocks. I'm hopefully back in training on Monday, I need to do sprint work not run 10 times around a fucking track."

Flynn said: "Well that's what he said..."

I turned to the physio and said: "That's right, isn't it? Sprints are better?"

He just sort of shrugged. I said to Flynn: "That's bollocks. Tell the manager I want to see him after."

I was raging but I did the 10 laps and went in and knocked on the manager's door. He answered and said: "Look, I've got a train to catch – can we talk Monday morning instead?"

I said: "Right, I'll speak with you Monday." I travelled back home and returned on Monday as arranged. I went straight to see him and carried on where I'd left off.

"What was all that 10 laps shit?"

He said: "Well you need to work on your fitness."

I said: "No, I need to work on sprints to get me ready to start full training again, so I'm fit and ready again."

He just said that he wanted me to do what he'd asked. I countered: "Right, well I just wanted you to know it's shit and the last thing I need right now."

He told me that was my opinion and that's where we left it.

I was living with Lucy in Swindon and leaving at half seven, arriving at nine and then leaving training and getting back for six. I was fucked and just going straight to bed. It was far from the genteel roll towards hanging my boots that up I'd imagined   I was working harder now than I had been when I was 18. Something had to give.

I returned to full training and had just finished my session when Tim rang to say Gary Mills, York City's manager, had called him to see if I wanted to go back and sign for them. Did I? I wanted to be there yesterday.

Taxi for Parky!

Brilliant! I'd be an hour from work, Oliver was around the corner and I'd enjoyed being at York so knew exactly what to expect. It was perfect. I knew Newport would let me go because of what had happened when Eastleigh had made an approach a few weeks before.

I told Tim it was a yes – 100 per cent yes – and to get me home. In fact, I'd said yes before I'd even spoken to Lucy about it, but she understood and realised it might be the last chance I had to move back home in my playing career. I went to see Graham Westley and told him, and he just said: "Right, no problem. Good luck."

It was just his training I didn't like, and we ended on good terms. As for me, I was heading back to the National League...

18

THE GRAND OLD DUKE OF YORK

I thought I'd got away with it until I got a call from the chairman on the coach home. I thought, 'Here we go,' but he said: "Jon, that is the best centre-forward performance I've seen in a very long time."

I knew I'd been selfish. I'd called Lucy and just said: "Look, I'm leaving. I'm going up to York to sign tomorrow." She asked whether there was going to be any discussion about it or what. In hindsight, it was a shit way to do things. She understood why I had to do it, as she always did, but the next day I packed and was heading back home for good.

Me living in Barnsley and Lucy living in Swindon was always going to be difficult because the only day I would be able to travel down to see her was Sunday, when I had Oliver. The only way things were going to work was if she came to live with me in Barnsley and, thankfully, she did.

It meant leaving her job as well as leaving her friends and family, but not long after I'd gone back, she moved in with me and decided to retrain as an air stewardess for Qantas instead. She has to do a lot of travelling as she's based at Heathrow, but that's what she did for me to allow me to live with my son. Lucy and Oliver get on a treat.

I'd agreed an 18-month deal with York to the end of the 2017/18 season. They were struggling and were second bottom of the table, so they'd be looking to me to find the back of the net on a regular basis to repay their investment.

Gary Mills had only just taken over and was assembling a squad he felt could keep the club up and I had been part of those plans.

The York fans were great with me. I think they understood one of the main reasons I'd left last time was financial and they seemed pleased to have me back. If only they'd known I walked over broken glass to go back!

I wasn't fit as my hamstring had stopped me playing much, but Millsy wanted me to play straight away and threw me in against Tranmere three days after signing. We lost 1-0 and I could see from that game that we weren't as bad as I'd first thought we might be. I'd always followed York's results over the years and had seen that season they'd had one or two batterings. I'd wondered what was going on at the club.

I loved Millsy straight away. He was proper old school and just class as a manager. The perfect manager for me, in fact. He'd soon got in the lads he wanted and we were there or thereabouts in every game we were playing.

We beat North Ferriby 1-0 on Boxing Day and then lost by the same score at their place five days later. Next up was Dover away and we travelled down on the Friday before the game and stopped at a pub on the way.

The lads who had come in with Millsy had told me what was going to happen and that we'd be going to the pub for a drink and food. Sure enough, we stopped at the pub they'd told me about and we went in. Millsy was already there, sat with a pint of Guinness in front of him.

He said: "Right, lads. If you want to have a drink, have one. Sausage and chip butties will be coming out in about an hour."

I thought I'd died and gone to heaven – it was as if somebody had decided to design a football club in my image. It was like a Carlsberg ad – "Footballs clubs aren't designed for Jon Parkin, but if they were…"

I said to anyone who was listening: "Erm… fuck it, I'll have a lager." I could see I was going to feel right at home in my second spell at York.

We were soon having skittles and darts tournaments and ended up having a brilliant afternoon. The only thing was, I came out of the pub pissed – as did two of the other lads. And we had Dover in less than 24 hours, who were up around the play-offs. To this day I don't know why I got sucked it into at the age 35. We got back on the coach and I was thinking, 'Christ, I might have overdone it a tad there.'

The warm-up at Dover was horrendous, with balls bouncing off knees and passes going anywhere but their intended target. I thought we might be in a spot of bother, especially as one of our centre-halves still looked pissed and, sure enough, we were 1-0 down after about four minutes.

I knew I'd messed up by having too many, but I was determined not to let Millsy down after he'd put his trust in us not to go mad. I ended up having a pretty good game, scoring in a 2-2 draw. If anything, I concentrated harder!

In fact, one of the lads had a great chance to win it in the last minute, but it was a decent point regardless. I vowed that on any future away trips we stopped at, it would be a couple of pints and no more.

I thought I'd got away with it until I got a call from the

chairman on the coach home. I thought, 'Here we go…' but he said: "Jon, that is the best centre-forward performance I've seen in a very long time."

I said: "Cheers chairman," and almost added: "I thought you were going to bollock me for being pissed up yesterday."

I'd learned my lesson though, and any away game we had down that end, I kept things under control and just had a couple of pints and no more.

We went on a bit of a run after that, winning eight and drawing eight of our next 19 games and I ended up with 14 goals. If we'd had that form all season, we'd have made the play-offs, but all the teams around us seemed to win when we did, and we just weren't pulling clear.

With about three games left, we'd got ourselves in a good position to stay up and we knew if we beat Wrexham at home, we'd have pretty much been home and hosed. I scored to put us ahead after two minutes, but we ended up getting dicked 3-1 against a side who had been struggling as well – but were now safe thanks to those three points when that should have been us.

It was a massive kick in the balls, but we went to Woking and got a 1-1 draw before our final game against Forest Green – it would have to be, wouldn't it?

We just needed to better Guiseley's result to stay up, while

I felt like I had a bit of a point to prove as well. Forest Green were already guaranteed a play-off spot but for the first 15 minutes or so, we just couldn't get anywhere near them. They went 1-0 up on six minutes. They were a possession team and just kept the ball. Their only failing was that, if anything, they overplayed it. Soon, one of their defenders was dispossessed by Simon Hislop, who crossed it in for me to make it 1-1.

At that stage, Guiseley were losing 1-0 to Solihull Moors and we were safe. But just before the break, Forest Green scored again so we went in 2-1 down at half-time. Millsy said to us: "Look, if we get a goal, unless you hear from us, we're safe."

We knew we had their measure and went out to give it a real go. Three minutes in, I made it 2-2 – a result that suited us both because we'd be safe, and Forest Green would get the point they needed to secure a second-leg play-off at home.

I obviously knew their captain Liam Noble from my time with the club, so around about the hour-mark, I went up to him and said that, at that stage, we were both alright. He said that he knew so I added: "Just tell your lads to relax and calm down a bit – we're both happy here."

There was still no word from the bench about Guiseley and it had turned into a bit of a training ground game with neither team really trying too hard. That said, we had a few great chances to win it, but their keeper Sam Russell pulled off about three worldies and I was like: "Fucking hell, Russler, give us a break, eh mate?"

The clock was ticking down and because we were live on BT Sport, we'd kicked off about five minutes later than everyone else. With three minutes left, we still hadn't heard anything official – but then we started hearing whispers from the crowd and it wasn't good.

Then the gaffer gets the message on that we now needed a goal. It turned out that Guisely had scored with almost the last kick of the game to make it 1–1, meaning that, as things stood, we were down.

We needed a goal but because we'd sort of wound down a bit thinking we'd done enough, it was hard getting going again. We never came close in the last five minutes and when the ref blew, we were relegated.

You could have dropped a pin inside Bootham Crescent and you'd have heard it. Even the Forest Green fans – a nice bunch as I'd mentioned previously – didn't celebrate or take the piss. There were about 4,000 fans in that day and everyone was just trying to absorb the fact that we'd slipped into the National League North for the first time in York City's proud history – a second successive relegation for the club who'd been a League Two side little more than 16 months earlier.

Relegation is a hard feeling to explain and it was only the

second time I'd experienced it, despite joining four clubs who had been looking down the barrel when I joined them.

Ironically, a few weeks before, we'd reached the FA Trophy final and would face my old club Macclesfield Town at Wembley. But because of the Football League play-offs, it wouldn't take place for another three weeks. Everyone was as flat as a pancake.

The gaffer thanked us all for our efforts and said: "Look, we've got the FA Trophy final in three weeks so I don't want you in until a week on Wednesday. If you want to go on holiday, go on holiday or do whatever you want to do. Let's go and win it and salvage something for our fans."

It was a bit of a nightmare scenario for me because it was my mate Jamie's wedding in Mexico and we'd been due to fly out on the Saturday – the day before the final, which was the Sunday after. And as best man, I sort of needed to be there!

He'd booked it especially late just in case we'd made the play-offs and final – but none of us had factored in the FA Trophy final. Not for the first time in my life I was asking, 'How's your fucking luck?'

I had to book a ticket for me and Oliver to fly out from

Gatwick on Monday instead with the wedding not until a few days after.

I'd already played at Wembley twice so I wasn't that arsed about it – I was happy for the lads who hadn't played there to get a chance. I found it hard to get my head around the game in all honesty after relegation, but we came back in for training and headed down to London for the match.

The best thing for me was that Oliver was one of the York City mascots and it ended up being a great day for everyone connected to the club. There was a crowd of around 38,000 there because the FA Vase had been on before us and some of those fans had stayed on to watch.

So I had my son holding my hand as we walked down the tunnel at Wembley and it's not something we'll ever forget.

It was the first time I'd started a game at Wembley but as soon as it began, it was obvious we were in for a tough 90 minutes. Macc were battering us from the off and for the first few minutes we hardly had a touch. But when we did get the ball, Danny Holmes managed to get a cross in, I glanced it to the left of the keeper and it flew in and put us ahead on eight minutes. A goal at Wembley aged 35 – well worth the wait – and it was right in front of our fans who were going nuts. It was also my 16th in 28 games that season.

It was a cracking game and we went in 2-2 at half-time, but

they were the better team and had been all over us for most of the half. We hadn't trained so much and they seemed to be in better shape than we were, so it was a long second half.

We clung on, cleared one off the line and with four minutes to go, the ball came to me. I hit it, it took a deflection but was going in until Aidan Connolly got there first to tap it home from a yard out. I didn't care who scored. The York fans went mad.

I was just relieved there was no extra-time because we were all blowing out of our arses by that point.

It turned out to be the winner – we won 3-2 and the FA Trophy made its way back to Bootham Crescent to end a disappointing season with something to celebrate.

I didn't really join in the party afterwards – I had Oliver with me and I just didn't want to. I was happy we'd won that game, but the fact was we'd slipped to the sixth tier of English football and it wasn't good enough. A club like York City deserve to be in the Football League.

Millsy told me he wanted to sign me on for another year but added that he wouldn't be able to pay me what he could have done if we'd stayed up. Pep Guardiola still hadn't called, so I was happy to sign and extend my career by another year.

I could have left if I'd really wanted to as there'd been interest from a few National League sides offering the same money I'd been on – or even a bit more. But I'd be 36 in December and besides, I was happy at York and wanted to help them get back up because I felt like I owed them. They'd restored my faith in football as a kid and then given me an escape from Newport, so I wanted to give them something back.

But if I'd thought some of the grounds in the National League had been bad, I hadn't seen anything yet...

19

OFF TO THE BREWERY

200 goals on the board – it was a good feeling and it got even better when I wafted a hopeful foot out as a low shot came in and it was enough to wrong-foot the keeper and win the game for us

You'd think going into a league that had grounds like The Brewery Field might have appealed to me, but for York City Football Club it was the last thing we wanted.

We started at home to Telford United and lost 1-0 with their keeper having a worldie and on another day we'd have scored five. I wondered whether that was how it was going to be during the 2017/18 season when York City rolled into town. Next up was Blyth Spartans and, not for the first time in my career, I hadn't a clue where we were heading. I was like: "Blyth? Spartans? Where the fuck is that?"

Don't get me wrong, it wasn't in a disrespectful way, I just genuinely hadn't a clue where they were. It wouldn't be the only time I asked that of our opposition that season.

We got to Blyth and their ground was little more than a sports and recreation club. It had been a bit of a shock going from the Football League to the National League but this was a real eye-opener because just five years earlier, I'd been on the bench away to West Ham United for Cardiff.

We knew we just needed to get our heads around the situation as a club and I needed to get my head around it as a player – not in some big time sort of way, either. We all just needed to give it our best. And we did.

The only thing at that level is you might be playing in front of 400 fans or fewer at some grounds and that meant you could generally hear everything that was being said. As you can imagine, it was rarely complimentary where I was concerned!

I've always got stick throughout my career wherever I've gone and I suppose at that level, I stood out even more. I got dog's abuse and if I'm honest, I quite like it. Wherever I've been, I've always been called a fat bastard or heard "Parkin you fat twat!" Nothing anyone could say bothers me. I just found it funny more often than not.

But when you're getting pelters in a crowd of 20,000 it's just lost in the general noise and it's easier to switch off – when there's a few dozen or just one bloke shouting from an otherwise empty stand, you can hear every word. As I say, it always makes me smile if truth be told.

I scored after 16 minutes against Blyth to get my season up and running but then pulled my hamstring on 31 minutes and was ruled out for a month. I bagged a couple against Spennymoor and it was around then that somebody pointed out that I was now on 199 career goals.

My first reaction was: "How has that happened? Not bad for a fat bastard from Barnsley." I'd never been one for stats, goals and appearances, but it was nice to know and if I was going to reach 200, I wanted Oliver to be there.

We played Stockport County and then Gainsborough Trinity at Bootham, but I didn't score in either game and missed a few chances I should have buried. Oliver didn't come to many away games but we had Salford City away in the FA Cup second qualifying round, so my dad, mum and brother took him along just in case.

We went 1-0 down but in the second half the ball came in and I stabbed it home to level it up. 200 goals on the board

– it was a good feeling and it got even better when I wafted a hopeful foot out as a low shot came in and it was enough to wrong-foot the keeper and win the game for us.

I set off to where Oliver was behind the goal but the York fans were going mad so I hastily moved on before he got crushed. He might remember it when he gets a bit bigger but I was just glad he was there to see it. It was a massive relief and I still couldn't get my head around it.

How had I managed that many goals? For a few moments afterwards, I was thinking, 'Christ, how many could I have scored if I hadn't gone out as much?' But that was a momentary thought – because it was more like, 'Nah, let's not go there! I've scored 200 goals and I've enjoyed myself so fuck it!'

That good feeling lasted until we were knocked out of the FA Trophy by South Shields and were seventh in the table and Millsy was sacked. I think we all felt we'd let him down because he deserved better. But that's the nature of football and if it's not happening on the pitch, it's usually the gaffer who pays the price.

Martin Gray left his post at Darlington and became our new

manager, but we just couldn't string the run of six or seven wins together we needed to get up there, drew too many games and lost against sides we shouldn't have.

Don't get me wrong, there were some good teams in that division with Darlington and Stockport County other clubs who had enjoyed better days not so long ago. We should have been pushing up in third or second at least and we weren't doing as well as the chairman had expected us to, or for that matter, as well as we the players had hoped to do.

We probably all could have done better. I was on 25 goals from 32 games and with a month or so to go, we were in fourth and on course for the play-offs with 11 games left, but my season was about to take a turn for the worse.

I was having a jog in training one morning and my knee basically collapsed from the back, which obviously wasn't good. I tried to carry on but it kept happening and I had to tell the gaffer I was going to have to go in and see the physio.

His face just dropped when I explained what had happened and said I'd need to have a scan. It turned out all the floating cartilage in my knee was clogging up the joint and causing it to collapse so I needed another clear-out and my cartilage trimming.

It was all but the end of my season as I underwent a knee op, but in our last eight games we won just once, drew two and lost five. There was still an outside chance we could make the play-offs on the final day so I said I'd be okay for the bench against Brackley Town. In reality, I was a good two weeks off being fit to play but I wanted to help if I could.

We needed to win and hope two other games went our way. At half-time we were drawing 0-0 and the other sides were both losing. We were in with half a chance, but when Brackley went 1-0 up after 52 minutes, the gaffer told me I was going to have to go on. I wasn't at my mobile best but I managed to hold off a challenge and nod the ball past the keeper for what we thought was an equaliser, but the ref disallowed it for a foul. It was never a foul in a million years and they ended up scoring again and that finished our season.

We'd dropped like a stone and ended in eleventh, five points outside the play-offs to complete York City's worst-ever season.

20

INTO EXTRA-TIME

Looking back, if I'd trained harder in pre-season, maybe drank less, who knows where I could have ended up? If I was given the chance of doing it all again tomorrow, would I do it differently? Nah

Paul Cox at Guiseley enquired about my availability during the 2017/18 season and, as a result, York offered me another year for the 2018/19 season – my 20th as a professional footballer.

I had no intention of leaving the club. As I see it, I owe York City a hell of a lot and it's very much a case of unfinished business. The York fans have been fantastic, and they keep turning up at home and travelling to away games in numbers, despite the shit last few seasons we've had. If this is to be my last season – and I hope it isn't – I want to help them get promoted and reach the 250-goals mark. If I can do that, we should be there or thereabouts come next May.

In December 2018, I'll turn 37 and I'll just have to see how my knee stands up going forward. The surgeon on my last op told me I'd need a new knee by the time I was 50 – and that was without even looking at the scan! I said: "Oh, that's good news then!"

He said he could do an operation that would delay that by maybe five years, but that would involve trimming a bit of my hip bone and knocking into my knee. I'll see how that goes. What I don't want is to get to the stage where I can't run around the back garden with Oliver – I don't get paid enough to take those sorts of risks any more.

If I can keep doing a job, scoring goals and enjoying it, I'll go for as long as I can. As I say, I'd love to help York get back up into the National League at least so that will be my aim for 2018/19. We move into the new 8,000-seater York Community Stadium next season, so there's added incentive to start at our new home in a new division and keep the feel-good factor going.

York are a league club who have just been in a rut but the future is looking a lot brighter and if we win promotion, I'd consider it as big an achievement as it was getting Stoke to the Premier League.

The thing is, it's getting tougher all the time. Because there are so many foreign players in English football, there's been a knock-on effect for clubs trying to get back into the Football League. There are players in the Championship who are good enough for the Premier League, players in League One good enough for the Championship and so on.

If you can get £700 playing for Accrington Stanley or £1000 playing for York, you'll choose York – and there's plenty of players of a certain age doing just that. If you are 21 to 25, you've still got a chance of kicking on, so Accrington makes more sense, but if you're 30 or more, you've already had a go and there isn't much scope to move upwards. So you have to think of your wage packet first and foremost. That's exactly what I did when I moved to Forest Green, though it turned out to be one of the best things I could have done.

Looking ahead, I've got one or two irons in the fire with an eye on years to come. I've started my coaching badges and I wouldn't mind a crack at management at some stage, see how I get on and see what it's like on the other side of the fence. I'd rather be a manager than a coach, I think, but it's a cut-throat business so we'll see.

I started doing a podcast with my old housemate and Preston

and Doncaster team-mate Chris Brown in 2018. He called me out of the blue and said he was thinking of doing a podcast and asked me if I would be interested in being a guest.

I said no problem. I didn't know much about it but I went along, did the first one which went well, and afterwards was asked to be on the panel full-time. I said: "Aye, that would be as grand as eggs."

We finished our first series of 'Undr the Cosh' in the summer of 2018 and our World Cup reaction videos on YouTube have had more than a million views, so watch this space.

I wouldn't mind a dabble in the media but I'll need to see how the management bit goes first. I like the idea of being paid to watch football and then chatting about it. That said, I love the banter side of it, too, and podcasts give you the licence to say what you want and have a laugh. If anyone listens to the podcasts we've already done, I doubt I'll ever get a job in management – unless it's someone who knows me! Let's see.

As for me and Lucy, we're happy and settled in Barnsley. She has long drives to London, then long flights with Qantas, so she can be doing 20-hour days. That side of things could be a lot easier for her but hopefully things will even out in years to come.

When she's away, I often spend time with her birthday present, Betsy. I'd asked her what she'd wanted for her birthday and she said she'd like a dog. I told her how tiring dogs were, but she said: "I'll look after it, I'll look after it!"

Her mum and dad had got a cat from a Romanian rescue charity called Paws2Rescue, so Lucy had a look on there and spotted Betsy, a whippet-cross. I said it was a scrawny thing and had seen another one – but it was her birthday and so we adopted Betsy. Naively, I thought Lucy would take the lead, so to speak, but as I suspected, it's dickhead here who ends up looking after Betsy most of the time. She's as good as gold, in fairness, and it would be strange without her.

I'm not quite ready to call it a day on my playing career and if these old knees hold up, I'll keep going. I've scored well over 200 goals in a career that began 20 years ago so I've no intention of leaving football behind any time soon. Looking back, if I'd trained harder in pre-season, maybe drank less, who knows where I could have ended up? If I was given the chance of doing it all again tomorrow, would I do it differently?

Nah...